HERE

Poems & Stories

by **Don McIver**

Hercules Publishing
Albuquerque, New Mexico, USA

ISBN: 979-8-218-75470-9
Release Date- 9/05/2025
Book design by PW Covington

Table of Contents

Foreword

Speeches become feats of brute force.
Mind over body.
The fight instinct on full-blast,
and pummeling them with

WORDS
        biting and abrasive
WORDS
        offensive and abused
WORDS
        sincere or sarcastic
WORDS
        memorized and rehearsed
WORDS
        mumbled and whispered . . .

Words become a poem
the poem becomes a poet,
a messenger of words.

This is the finale of the first poem I ever heard by Don McIver.

The summer of 2002 was a hot one. So, it makes sense that it was then, I began my obsession with poetry. I was sixteen years old and just happened to be awake at

11:30 on a Sunday night, scanning the radio stations on my old boombox. The dial picked up a signal at 89.9, and a soon-to-be familiar voice caught me by surprise. "Is that a poem on the RADIO?!"

I always kept a blank tape in the cassette player for moments like this. I have archives of random snippets of songs and DJ banter caught on 90-minute Maxwells, whenever I hit the record button at just the right second.

I let the tape run, as this random radio show kept throwing some bangers through the speakers. A Saul Williams poem next. Then comedy from Bill Hicks. A poem by Kate Makkai. Patricia Smith after. "The Revolution Will Not Be Televised," ended the set. And the DJ spoke. "Tune in next Sunday for The Spoken Word Hour. I'm Don McIver. Thanks for listening."
And I said, "You're welcome, Don!" Laughing to myself as I talked to my stereo.

In September, my friends told me about this Friday night poetry slam at the

Blue Dragon Coffeehouse, just up the street from Albuquerque High School. It was the kind of place my grandparents would have never let me go, if they didn't have their assumptions that poetry and coffee shops were harmless. This place had emo and goth kids on the front patio, smoking hookahs and poorly-rolled joints of schwag. About 100 people crammed into a performance space that could maybe fit 40 people in the afternoon. I remember the pool table in the back room, the smoking section back when those were still a thing. Teenagers passing around bottles of Fruitopia topped with Vodka. The coffee shop owner was on the mic, an old hippie playing a homemade drum and throat singing. Pretty funky place for a catholic boy from Old Town to end up on a Friday night.

The open mic was wrapping up as I put my name down on the poetry slam sign-up list, which had about 22 names on it already. A couple minutes went by, and the emcee made the announcement over the crowd, "All slammers meet me outside for the draw!" I had no idea what those words in that sentence meant when strung together, but I recognized that voice. It was the dude from the radio show! He explained the rules and all the poets drew numbers from a hat. I drew last, and Don said something about the luck of the draw. The show began, and poets took their 3 minutes on stage, while the slam judges tanked all those poets' dreams of winning the $20 first prize and a chance to qualify for the Albuquerque Poetry Slam Team. I made it to the final round of the slam. My turn came up, and I fuckin' rocked, man! The energy of that crowd left me feeling like a rock star! The final line of my poem hit hard, and the applause followed me until I got back to my seat at the counter.

Then the scores came in: 7.0, 7.9, 8.2, 9.9, 10. I got 3rd place in my first ever poetry slam. 2nd place went to Danny Solis. 1st to Tony Santiago.

Don called me up to the stage to collect my consolation prize. A coupon for a free meal & drink from the Blue Dragon, and a copy of the Albuquerque Poetry Slam Grand Slam Championship CD. He told me matter-of-factly, "That was your first slam?! Come back next month."

With that simple encouragement, I was hooked on poetry slam. I hit up every show in town that year, and Don was at every one of them. As a competitive poet, Don had an approach to strategy that was unmatched. It was a way of picking the right poem at the right moment in the right crowd. Read the room, he'd say.

Fast forward to 2004, and I made my way through the City Championship tournament and was alternate on the Albuquerque Poetry Slam Team, at just 18 years old. While not a full team member, I still showed up to every rehearsal at the Harwood Arts School, just a 10-minute walk up Mountain Road from my house, and across the street from Don's. He became a close friend, always had my back and kept me on the right path. He's one of the few poets to have met my whole family: my grandparents, aunts and uncles, and cousins who aren't around anymore.

In August of 2004, the slam team piled into a 15-passenger van headed for the National Poetry Slam in St. Louis. In the backseat, he reached into the cooler and pulled out a can of PBR. He passed it to me and said something like, "So you graduated from high school, and I'll never be your substitute teacher. Have this. You earned it," and I drank my first ever beer on the front end of a 16-hour road trip. How many hundreds of adventures can two poets have in a lifetime?

When I read this book, I can see all the scenes like a movie in my mind. A film set along the streets of Albuquerque, of America after the war began, from Manhattan to Baghdad. Streets that don't look how they do today, but how they'll always be in my memories. I see the bag lady with her ice cup as she makes her daily pilgrimage up Central Avenue. I see the SWAT teams laying beatdowns on the No War protestors on Johnson Field. I see a man wearing a dress, riding his bicycle across town for a drag show, and surviving to tell the story. I see the dumpster fires lit in the days after the police brutality marches. Each poem, a scene from the Duke City too recent to be history, and too long ago to be "just the other day."

"Some people need a Green-Card to live in the US," I always joked, "and some people need a Brown-Card to live in Albuquerque." And Don McIver is a poet who earned his Brown-Card in my book. My city is just like my family. When we see that you're all-in, for not only the good times but the struggles as well, you're in for life. Por Vida.

23 years have gone by since I heard Don on the radio, since I met him at that smoked out coffeehouse, since we embarked on the first of many poetry road trips together. On those long drives, he often told me of his obsession with the Beat Generation, especially Kerouac's *On the Road*, a book I'd never read if Don hadn't nagged me into it.

Once I read it, I finally understood. The miles a poet puts under their wheels and heels are what makes the words a poem; the poem, a poet; a messenger of words.

-Damien Flores

The City of Albuquerque's 7th Poet Laureate

Ramblin' Man

for Dickie Betts

By the time I graduated high school, I'd
already had sixteen different
addresses,
in ten different towns,
in three states,
with a state between each one.

Let's just say, my old man was "trying to
make a living and doing the best he
[could,]"
which was often not quite good enough.
So, we'd pack what we couldn't give
away and take the too-full moving van
to where sometimes my mom had
family,
and sometimes my dad did, too.
We didn't have time to say goodbye, let
alone hope they'd understand.

In motels, if I unload my suitcase too
quickly into empty dressers,
and hide the luggage
behind the ironing board
to make it feel like home,
it's cause
that's what home feels like,

if you're the son of a ramblin' man.

If I use milk crates for shelves,
hold on to empty boxes
and give stuff away too soon,
it's cause why move shelves when an
empty crate will do?
why search for boxes when it's time to
go?
and why hold onto things you no longer
need or want?
That's what it feels like when you're son
of a ramblin' man.

When the choice to move became mine,
I moved to Albuquerque.
And the city let me know what I was
worth
and for some reason wouldn't let me
leave.

By the time the city said that I was free
to go,
I loved it so much I chose to stay.
Albuquerque,
the city where I found my clan and
donned the colors with a smile.
Albuquerque,
when everyone is dancing with
everyone, that means you've found a
home.

My parents taught me that family was
where I'd find it or bind it,
and if I didn't see it, it's 'cause I was too
blind to see.

Preface

This poem is for Thornton Wilder and is
called, "Living for the City."
It was written by Don McIver.
The white poet watches from a window
as a roadrunner runs
under a bush and jumps up on the
outside table.

The outside table is spotted black from
the mulberry tree above it.
Looking at the table, he hears the public
address system from the minor league
baseball stadium.
A mile away they announce the score,
again,
yet he won't be able to understand it.

In this poem,
he lives close enough to know that they
are giving the score,
but just far enough away to not be able
to make out what it is specifically.

This morning, his first stop was many
people's grocery store of last resort: a 7-
11 on Central,
the main street of this town.

It's where the people in this poem go
when they're too tired to tolerate Smith's
for toothpaste or half and half.
Recently re-modeled, they sell
cigarettes out a side window between
midnight and five A.M.

He bought a house in this hood and
became one of three owner-occupants
on the block.
His neighbors next door, Latina and
Jewish own their place too but don't
seem to be there during the day, any
day.

Two doors down,
the only time the native American
neighbor seems to be at home is
weekends, always by himself, always
working on something:
windows, truck repair, weed pulling.

Three doors down
four other poets occupy the house and
two of the three studios out back.

She's biracial and he's biracial, and they
fight yet keep the fights to themselves
as the biracial poet shares his internet
with the teacher-poet,

whose porch backs up to Wendy's.

In this poem,
the teacher-poet can order Wendy's
drive-through from his porch.

Next to them is a subdivided house, now
triplex, and is mostly empty most of the
time because the Asian landlord has
really high standards.

Even further down this rundown house
welcomes traveling musicians. The
white hipsters advertise through some
network,
so bands book shows in the rundown
house's living room.

Cars get ticketed for not having a permit
and sometimes wrap around the block
as late-night conversations always wake
him up.
Their voices become background noise
to the busy thoroughfare.

This is the slow reveille of the city
waking up to the employee traffic
from the two nearby colleges less than 6
blocks away.

It's not uncommon that the poet finds
himself at both on any given day of any
given week.

No one lives in this neighborhood long
as the empty spaces ebb and flow with
registration and financial aid.

He'll fix broken ottomans and take
couches off curbs as often
as he'll leave tennis shoes, broken
shelves, and logs of Chinese Elm.
All are gone by the end of day.

He minds a trash can at the corner;
even though people use it even when
it's full.

His overgrown bamboo obstructs the
view of the traffic up ahead,
even though it has caused a fine.

People walking by throw their cigarette
butts on his lawn
and ditch illegal drugs upon occasion.

The folks living on the street never ask
for change
but will stop him a block away as if their
worksite is Route 66

and until they're on it, they are simply off
the clock.

This is the world he calls home
and it feels like it should almost all the
time.
He can eat almost any type of food with
just a few steps.
The bartenders at the nearest bars
know him by name;
The regular clientele acknowledges him
as he walks in
still dressed from work.

Nice neighborhood, you know what I
mean?
It's always alive, and he loves this prime
spot he calls home.
The trash gets picked up on time and
the mail is always in its box.

He sometimes wants to be remarkable;
sometimes wants to see his name in
lights,
but most times he just wants to write,
and sometimes just holds the pen above
the paper not sure he has anything
to say.

Neighborhood

the lowered pickup trucks
the booming cabs
the teens, the greasy haired, Raiders
capped teens
are flashing you signs,
gang signs

Gray
out of state
vans
drop black and brown women
on anonymous corners.
Money's changed hands.
Was it a blow-job or a fuck?

Yellow oak leaves swirl around brown
puke and blood.
Everything
but the oak leaves
belongs to a kid that died
the night before.

Cadillacs, Econo-vans, and Jeeps
smiling and leering
crave more than a stare.
Rendezvous on a side street
and they'll want you to, "Go for a ride."

Can't see out the back window?
The window's not that dirty.
Shattered,
the hole in the corner belongs to a
bullet.
Bits of glass plunge on potholes and
bumps.
Puny panes of rotten luck line the curb
and the street.

Did I leave the keys in the car?
Did I drive it way,
launch it over a cliff,
into the river and through the woods?
or just plain forget where I parked it?
You can't believe they'd steal it.
Not your car,
Not that car,
Yet it's gone.
Someone you rapped with would give
you a break.
And he wants to as he bashes your skull
with a pipe.
He wants you to fight.
Calls you a liar, a coward, an ass.
You'd do anything to make him go
away:
Plead, rap, give him your bike for safe
passage.
Anything.

The Territory

for Robert Frost

No bigger than a housecat,
a small gray roadrunner has adopted
our neighborhood.
Almost any morning, I can spot him.
Sometimes up the road a bit,
turned towards the sun with his feathers
spread apart, warming up,
or just bouncing from our fence to our
roof,
then over the top and down to the other
fence
that keeps our lot separate from our
neighbor's.

I wonder if he recognizes me,
knows how I know his colors:
the red and white stretched out from
behind his eyes like mascara
how I recognize his stuttered step,
his head ducked down so his beak is the
first thing impacted
on anything that doesn't get out of his
way.

Strange how the cats don't seem to
bother him,
and I wonder what he eats,

and whether I should spread some bird
seed on the wall.

My neighbor and I exchange
pleasantries
and stay in our respective territories--
a smaller part of his territory—
a neighborhood in the middle of the city.

Answer Me That

I'm sitting in a coffee shop on
Central, and I'm a little shocked by what
I just saw on the walk over. A white
truck with a black dog in the back was
hit and spun around ninety degrees.
The dog became a cartwheeling bundle
of black fur twisting and turning in the air
for a good twenty feet. None of the
people were harmed and the cars, good
old disposable cars, who cares? But the
dog? He trotted back to the truck and
jumped into the bed like nothing
happened.

Now I can't get this image out of
my head: this black mass twisting and
turning in the air, and I couldn't stop and
say I was a witness because I kept
seeing this black mass that I didn't even

realize was a dog at first and I'm glad I didn't see him hit pavement and I'm supposed to write about Kerouac. I'm supposed to write about disjointed style and verbal barrage of Kerouac and Beat Generation when I can't help but shake and freak out. AHHHHHH!

Take this image from my mind Jack; take it with you on the road and you and Neal, Cody, Dean can mull it over and talk how grand it is as you plow the eternal present of 40's America. And I wonder if you could write fast enough Jack; I wonder if the very act of writing counter to Zen because you are having to absorb the world and spit it back out. Then why write, Jack? Why write? Answer me that.

The Meandering River

My parents chose the neighborhoods
carefully: near parks,
good schools, quiet streets. Most of the
time they succeeded
from afar in finding the right fit, but
circumstances being what
they were, two years later we moved
again.

Finally, when I was fifteen, they stopped
upending the whole family
and stuck, at least, with the same school
even though by the time I'd graduated
we'd moved to four different places in
the same school district. At least
I got to stick with pretty much the same
group of friends for a while.

As adults, I and all my siblings have
stayed rather rooted since we've
been on our own. I've lived in a variety
of places all over Albuquerque
for the last thirty years, but now find
myself just passing the eleven year
mark in this house, a block from one of
the busiest streets in town. It's a house,
but the living is urban, as most of the
places up and down the street have

been carved into duplexes or triplexes,
and one of the old churches
has become Single Room Occupancy
with clientele that hangs out
on their corner smoking cigarettes and
talking. Every morning,
one of the men from the SRO walks up
our street. He's tall, with a short cut
of white hair and big fox tail of a white
mustache and a wild bush
of a white goatee. Usually smoking a
cigarette, he'll nod when he passes by.

This morning as we were about to leave,
my wife realized she'd forgotten
something.

He'd just passed by, and as she undid
her seatbelt, he stopped
in front of our house. He wavered a bit
and stood there. Suddenly he begin
urinating on the bush, a Texas Ranger,
in front of our house.

"I guess I'll wait a bit." We watched as
he relieved himself. A river of urine
poured forth, mostly on the sidewalk but
some on the Texas Ranger, too.
It went on and on, but finally, he zipped
up. She got out and went back inside,

stepping over the urine that meandered
to the street
and the street grate.

I watched as he staggered across the
street, meandering and zig-zagging in
that way that intoxicated people do, one
block, then another, then finally
disappearing into the SRO.

Broken Glass

Our detached garage borders
a busy, weekday thoroughfare.
The south facing front of our
house opens to a side street.
From the house, we can't
see the garage door.

Weekend chores commence
with conversation over
coffee: pick up after the dog,
sweep the floors, grocery
shopping, meal planning, laundry
then the inclusion of periodic
and unique chores:
pick up trash that gets thrown
onto our driveway from the busy,
weekday thoroughfare,
replace the broken glass
from a framed photo
that tumbled off a cabinet
to the ground when I
bumped it, and fix the bedroom
light fixture.

Today, the driveway
can use its clean-up:
Scraps of paper, newsprint,
disposable coffee cups,

to-go bags, and a picture
frame. There's no photo
in the frame, but the glass
is not broken. It fits.
The bedroom light fixture
will have to wait.

Don't Forget to be Awesome

This year is brought to you by
Diet Dr. Pepper, two
junk bikes, a broken
display cabinet, a ditched
leather purse holding random
keys and a Nintendo Flipnote,
a pressurized stock pot,
a wine glass, and a coffee
mug with "Don't Forget to be Awesome"
emblazoned on the front.
Such are the discoveries
in my neighborhood
this morning,
as we set out to walk the dog
and wish our friends "Happy New Year!"

We didn't make it
to midnight, so sometime
after ten someone threw
the bikes over our fence
such that one of them
was hanging from the lower
branches of our mulberry tree

while the other just rested
on the path to the front door
as if they walked up

and meant to knock,
which they didn't.

Then upon opening the gate,
a twelve pack of Diet Dr. Pepper
sat on the steps. One was missing,
so now we had an eleven pack.
Unfortunately, I don't drink Diet
Dr. Pepper (which doesn't prevent them
from sponsoring the rest of the year).

As for the purse, it was sitting
under a parked car and had the keys
and Flipnote in it, but no other
identifying mark.

Farther down the road,
someone put the pot,
the wine glass,
and coffee mug on the sidewalk
to be picked through,
so we obliged.

Now soaking and sanitizing
I think of Robert Hunter's
"...one man gathers what another man
spills."
Indeed.

Howl: the "Neighborhood Clean-up Day" Edition

for Allen Ginsberg

Part II.
What beast of remote-control fingers
and plastic destruction toppled the
recycling bin and dumped its contents
onto the street?

Moloch! Desperation! Litter!
Monstrousness! Recycling bins and
windy spring days! Cups flattened by
cars! T-shirts soaking up gutter water!
Old boxes marked by tire tracks!

Moloch! Moloch! Daymare of Moloch!
Moloch the homeless! Hungry Moloch!
Moloch the hangover of Saturday
morning!

Moloch the discarded wrappers! Moloch
the burned-out nooks in alleyways and
Congress of hunger!

Moloch whose buildings are empty!
Moloch the trash ending up in empty
lots! Moloch the garbage truck and
overflowing dumpsters!

Moloch the neighborhood association!
Moloch whose business is everyone
else's! Moloch whose fingers
are wrapped around the handle of a
thirty-two-inch trash picker! Moloch
whose nodding heads are staring at
fenced yards! Moloch whose yards are
unkempt! Moloch whose ear is a street
racing car!

Moloch whose eyes are boarded-up
buildings! Moloch whose breast is an
abandoned church! Moloch whose
historic houses stand on the tree lined
street like registered monuments!
Moloch whose drive-through windows
belch car exhaust and over full grease
bins!

Moloch whose love is cracked asphalt
and uprooted concrete! Moloch whose
soul is pitch covered telephone poles!
Moloch whose poverty is the drug dealer
on a BMX bike! Moloch whose fate is a
litter strewn driveway! Moloch whose

name is the neighborhood association!
Moloch in whom I type emails!

Moloch in whom I meet neighbors!
Fearful in Moloch! Dunkin' Donuts in
Moloch! Wendy's and a headshop in
Moloch! Moloch who entered this
morning early! Moloch in whom I am
patrolling the streets! Moloch who left
me straddling a pile of trash looking for
needles but found only feces! Moloch in
alleys as bathrooms!

Moloch! Moloch! Annual clean-up day!
Recycling from my bin! Disposable
artifacts as treasures! Pages from an
open mike! Names on a page! My
handwriting!

They lost their voices reciting this poem!
Recycling bins, black plastic, crab grass
and tumble weed lifting the city to
dumpsters which exists and are
everywhere around us!

Paper! Cups! Yarn balls! T-shirts! CD
cases! A list of readers on an open
mike! Two blocks away!
Gone down the Gold Street gutter that
drains to the river!

Civilization! Neighborhoods! Apartment complexes! Small businesses! Break ins! Under the bush! Surgical masks and tissue paper! Pushed here by wind!

Real holy nodding heads! They grabbed it all! The people walking through! The revving engines! They found the script! A page of Ginsberg's poem lost on the wind! Down to the juniper! Crumpled in the roots!

Suite: 4 Days of Car Trouble

1. Jumper Cables
After work,
I turn down the street
And notice a beat-up white car
In my usual parking space
With the hood up.
As I turn into my gate,
A young woman hops out of the car.
"Do you have jumper cables?"
I do, and jump her, and she's on her
way.

2. Jumper Cables
Out the door to get to a class,
Another white car, hood propped open.
Young woman stops me.
"Can you give a me jump?"
I can, and try, but no luck.

3. Hot Wired
Morning coffee, front porch
And I notice a black mini van
Running with its rear hatch open
Parked in front of my friend's old truck.
A few minutes later I hear some grinding
noise

38

And see the hood on his truck pop open.
Curious, I walk down there to see if he
needs help.
The truck is running; the mini-van owner
closes his rear hatch
And pulls away.
I look at the truck and open the driver's
door.
The minivan turns around and drives
slowly back my direction.
I say to his closed window, "This isn't
your car."
In the cab, the truck has been hotwired
and now idles.
No way to turn it off, I call my friend and
tell him someone
Tried to steal his truck.

4. Subaru
The niece is in town for Spring Break.
Arranged ahead of time, she's going to
borrow
Her grandmother's Subaru while in town
And take it south to visit the sights.

A phone call.
They are on the side of the road.
They heard a thump, then smoke,
Then pulled over. Car wouldn't start
again
And flames burst from the hood.

Abandoned car, flames took over.
Clothing, cooler, laptop, Subaru all
gone.

    5. Catalytic Converter
An hour of classical music and spoken
word.
A weekly show just north of downtown.
Driving beat-up, old truck because niece
has the car.
Afterwards, walk out,
Hop behind the wheel.
Notice truck is louder than usual.
While inside the show, somebody cut
catalytic converter off.
In just the hour I was inside.

The Souped-up Car

"I regard the theater as a serious business, one that makes or should make man more human, which is to say, less alone."
-Arthur Miller

Scene One
Biking up the hill from downtown:
side streets, shortcuts through
driveways
and underpasses. Late night, bus stops
lit
up but mostly empty and on now our
street.
Squealing tires smoke up ahead and
we hear a car rev up and race until
it's at the corner ahead of us. Too much
machismo; too little to do in a souped-up
car
and he squeals a U-turn and heads the
other
way. Crossing the street, we're home.

Scene Two
Two young women sit up against the
fence
in our dark driveway. They look up.
Three
short sentences: "Turn it off, please. I
don't

want him to see. Can you turn off your lights
please?" She, brunette hair braided down
the right, a smattering of teardrop tattoos
dot her right cheek. A blonde-haired friend sits next to a small suitcase. "Do you need to use our phone?"
"No. We're just really scared and don't want him to see us."
"We have to get in that garage."
She nods.
"You can stay here if you want."
She nods.
"You want us to call the cops?"
"No, please.   But if you had some water?"

Scene Three
Garage opens but the burnt-out light from the opener has never been replaced.
The drive stays dark, and if they don't move he might not see them. We give them a bottle of water then shut the door.
I hang out in our yard and watch the souped-up car circle round the block a couple of times before it finally exits.

The Neighbors

1. Target Practice

Jolting us awake at what I later learned
was 11:30,the gunshots were fired off in
rapid succession. We both sat up as our
dog snuck out of the bedroom and into
the back room to disappear under my
desk. I got up and peered out my front
window, waiting for sirens, but it stayed
silent the rest of the night.

Hearing gunshots is not uncommon.
It is Albuquerque after all.

The next morning I'm walking my dog
when a neighbor stops me and asks if
I'd heard the gunshots.
"I can never tell
where they come from," I tell him. Our
bedroom window faces our neighbor's
drive, and any noise just seems to
come
from everywhere, so I always assume it
is coming from the major intersection
just a block away. "It's not," he says.
"It came from the parking lot. Behind my
house."

An hour later, I'm walking down the street with my morning coffee in hand when I see a cop car pulled over in front of another neighbor's house. That neighbor, across the street, is standing on the sidewalk and waves me over. "You hear the gunshots?" I nod, and he looks at his Range Rover, parked on the street between my two cars. "Let me show you."

He shows a video captured by his neighbor's doorbell. It's three young men, kids really, jumping a gate between the two properties. One of them carries a gun. "A Tech 9," he says, then looks at his Range Rover again, which I finally notice has been hit. His passenger window is shattered but remains in place; the side mirror has been hit as well.
"I was so out of it 'cause of my Ambien that I didn't hear a thing.
I've been waiting for the cops since five A.M." I look at his car, the video, then my cars parked in front and behind his.

It is Albuquerque after all.
So, luck is sometimes just a matter of waking up.

This morning an email from the first
neighbor has just a simple subject line,
"Alley Shooting." I look at the attached
video, and it's three young men, kids
really, walking across the street and
standing in the sensor activated light
from his parking lot facing garage. One
of them turns toward the street, and
then you see three quick bursts of light.
He hands something to another one of
the young men, kids really,
and he shoots three quick times as
well. They talk, though there is no
audio, then run back across the street to
the alley
behind my neighbor's house. I don't
even think they realized what they hit, or
could've hit in the houses across six
lanes
and a row of parked cars.

Hearing gunshots is just a matter of
waking up,and luck is not uncommon.
It is Albuquerque after all.

   2. The Shootout at Wendy's

We turned on the closed-captioning
even though the stereo was loud.

Not wanting to miss the bad mix
of dialogue and background music,
we also like to get the full effect
of whatever we're watching
on our own version of a big screen.

<<If I'd written this earlier, I'd probably
incorporate more of White Noise into it
cause that is what we were watching,
but I've been sitting on this poem…
for
a while
now.>>

Lots of water dropped
in lots of hot oil-
-a burst of gunfire.
We looked at each other
then went back to watching.

The red and blue lights pierced
our window, and we paused
the…
movie.

A police car blocked
traffic heading north
and a cop waved traffic
away from the…
scene.

A brick wall separated my
backyard from the sidewalk.
A few more cop cars,
an ambulance,
and a paramedic
were stopped in the three
northbound lanes
faced…
the wrong way,
next to my wall.

Two young men, face
down on the pavement,
moved, but one was being
treated by the paramedic.

Inside then out the back door,
where, by standing on a bench,
I saw what was happening.

<<If I'd written this earlier, I'd be able to
tell you what color of clothes they wore
and if they were writhing in pain, but I've
been sitting on this poem…
for
a while
now.>>

They let the first kid up.
The second kid's pants
are down around his knees

exposing his upper thighs
where the paramedic
is cleaning what is clearly
a bullet wound in his right one.

Back at the corner,
the cop talked with
a woman and a tall young man.
The woman explained
that the kid who's been shot
was her son, and can she
and her other son, his brother,
check on him.

The cop held his hands out,
keeping them from walking by him.
Another cop came up.
They gesticulated at this new cop,
and the son, emphatic enough
that I can make out what he said,
"She's his mom."

I turned back and talked
to my back neighbor,
who was standing below me
on the street.

A shootout at the Wendy's
behind his place,
and the kids ran down
to the street and hid.

One had been shot.
The shooters drove away.

Back in front, my neighbor
across the street tells me,
"They never did nothing
with the videos we had
of the shooting before,
and it's the same kids.
They're up to no good."

I walked with him to the cop,
and we told him about what
had happened three months before.

3. The Carjacking

"What a dumbass," my feed explodes
with a picture of a young man standing
next to a BMW sports car.
"It's a failed carjacking.
If you know who this is,
please let APD know."

I don't but read the story.
The kid in the picture tried
to carjack the BMW, but it
didn't work.

Then he tried to take the cell phone

away from the driver who was taking
his picture, and that is what I'm looking
at now.
The driver is fine.

"If you know who this is, please
let APD know." It could be any
number of young men I see
every day:
a red sweatshirt,
short curly brown hair,
the slightest hint of a mustache.
The carjacking fails 'cause the kid
didn't know to drive a stick.

4. The Standoff

Early afternoon and I approach my
street.
Down the street before mine,
I see a police car diverting traffic east
'cause the northbound lane is blocked
off.

At my street, a cop tells me I can't get
home.
I stand at the corner until another cop
over the bullhorn says,
"You in the red jacket," meaning me,
"That is not a safe location.
You need to move along."

I text some neighbors,
tell them they can't come home,
talk to a cop about closing the alley
to the north too, as many places
can be accessed via the alley.
"We are just trying to serve a warrant.
If you are inside, we are only interested
in apprehending the one person.
Come out, and we won't have to call
the SWAT team. They will come in
if you don't come out."

A few minutes later I watch the kid –
caught on the camera playing
with a gun months before,
on the pavement face down
getting a bullet wound cleaned
by paramedics while I watched
White Noise, and caught
on a cellphone camera 'cause he
didn't know how to drive a stick –
walk backwards with his hands
in the air towards the cops.
He was wearing a red sweatshirt.

Dumpster Fire

I called the fire department because I
wanted them to drown an actual
dumpster fire.
I could not pinpoint the block where
the dumpster burned, yet know my
address is on the same block.

Then, when the 9-1-1 operator asked
me
to identify the cross-streets, I only
remembered three out of four.

In the moment it felt like I'd stumbled
upon a dumpster fire in a foreign town
not one in my actual neighborhood.

Thus, when the fire department did
show up, I had to wave them down.
They had no idea what block, what
alley,
what dumpster or even what cross-
streets
housed a blazing dumpster fire and I
was left with directing them there.

I called the fire department because
I wanted them to put out an actual
dumpster fire.
Only, learning that my memory is the
real dumpster fire and the neighborhood
where it burns is in my head.

Street Fighting Man

*"Hey! Said my name is called disturbance
I'll shout and scream, I'll kill the king, I'll rail at all his
servants"*
-Mick Jagger and Keith Richards

Saturday night and I'm drinking,
enjoying
my house with friends and I'm inside
and outside when the phone rings. My
buddy went to visit our neighbor two
doors
down and someone was hovering by our
gate and took a swing as he walked by.

He'd like to come back but the dude is
still there.

I stand in my yard, just up some stairs
from our gate, and don't know what is
going on. Overgrown obstructed walk,
so
rather than go out that way, I go out
the back, across the street, and stare
back.
Some dude is standing on our walk,
shielded from the light by our
landscaping,
and he is gone, messed up, in a world
that's not like ours. He is shirtless and
walks

two steps, talks, then two steps back
then stands,
hovers, and walks, hovers, two steps,
talks,
hovers, almost trips, hovers, walks, two
steps, talks, hovers. He is married to
drugs and poverty.

So I call the cops…non-emergency, and
find
out that my buddy has called too. I
watch
and wait. Wait and watch. Shirtless
makes his way around the corner and
stands, head on chest, rocking, but not
passing out, then moves, rocks, still not
passing out but head resting on his
chest…a state of near sleep

So I call 9-1-1 and wait…
tell them that he might get hit by passing
cars.
A person walking towards him swings
wide
in the street, another walks right up to
him
and they walk off…a dealer with just the
right touch and words to get him
moving, and still no cops.

An hour later still no cops, and I'm
shutting the house down for the night;
no safer than the hour before.

A Four-Legged
Intersection

In line to pull a U-turn
at my intersection,
two guys talk smack
through open windows
from their cars,
then speed up the busy,
weekday thoroughfare
to stop adjacent at the
next intersection.

A shirtless man
walks up the median.
Both arms extended upward,
he thrusts everyone the finger.
He barks at the two guys
talking smack as they pass
him by. He walks north
into the middle of the busy
intersection, then circles
back to the median
before crossing the street
to a grassy hill on the corner.

A few minutes later,

he's standing on the median
again and barking obscenities
at people passing by.

He drifts over to the grassy hill,
on the corner, lays down,
and when I bike by later
he's making out
with someone I never
even knew was there.

Disappear

for Skip Daniels

I.
What I have of yours:
three different sized hexes,
two Camalots,
one gear sling
and an odd assortment of carabiners.

What I remember of you:
nights on imagined cliff faces,
olive and onion pizza,
afternoon talk shows
and discussions about the nature of
mysticism
and epileptic seizures.

An all-but dissertation neural-
psychologist,
you were becoming increasingly
unraveled.

I, a teacher and a weekend rock climber
needed to replace the companionship of
an
eight year relationship.

You held the end
of my rope.

The ground was the last place that I
wanted to be.
My wings had been clipped, and still I
tried to be
the person I knew I would never be:
a boyfriend,
methodical
worker bee.

II.
You should've never climbed with me.
When you backed off,
I climbed up into the crack,
stitched the climb up behind me.
moving farther off the ground.
Stranding the gear in the crack in the
climb,
we were over our heads.
At first, several pieces
held
our
rope
in place
and then
thinking
we'd
find
another
way,
we pulled the rope down, too.
Our

gear
was
still
in
place.
Now our rope was down.
I looked up:
wired stopper,
2 Camalots,
medium-sized hex
and another wired stopper,
each with a carabiner
attached,
hung from the crack
that
we
tried
to
climb.

You weren't climbing anymore.
So, I,
novice climber,
depressed teacher,
heartbroken 30-something
had to pull my harness on one more
time.
trust my feet and shoes,
trust you to hold the rope,
as I climbed to the last piece.

My first lead:
cleaning the pieces that we'd set up,
moving to a wired stopper,
clipping in the rope,
then moving to a Camalot,
clipping in,
moving to another
Camalot,
clipping in,
moving to a medium-sized hex,
clipping in,
then to another wired stopper
and clipping in some 75 feet off the
ground.

At the top of the climb,
I laced
the rope
through
a bolt,
and
the wired
stopper,
then
rappelled
and cleaned all that gear.

III.
A week later you left a note,
saying you needed to take a "break"
from climbing.

Our last climb "freaked" you out.
And I was pissed:
You introduced me
to this sport that required two
and then
stranded me
with a taste for rock
that won't
go away.

IV.
A month later,
I was short some cash.
It was check number 459,
yet I wrote checks in the three
hundreds.
The bank said, "Pizza Hut."
And I thought, pizza?
Had I been so stoned
or drunk
that I didn't remember ordering food?
"Can you send me a copy of that
check?"
Two weeks later,
the check had yet to arrive.
You stopped
coming by my room
late at night.
Hospital collection agents started
calling,
and any food

in the kitchen
was disappearing.

I started buying meat
and chicken
and pork,
because I knew you wouldn't eat it.

I was in and out,
reading poetry,
seeing shows,
trying to replace a girlfriend
with just about any girl.

You were going crazy…
Starving yourself.
Sneaking in another room
and
stealing food.
Sneaking in my room
and
stealing my checkbook.
The xeroxed copy that I finally got
had a signature
that clearly
wasn't mine.
and then…
"Skip. This is Bill Lucero, your bail
bondsmen. I want to know
what happened."

V.
Your door had been locked for days.
Random noises came from
your room
late at night,
but the door was locked.

When Bill Lucero came by our house,
I assured him that you'd not been home.

Finally, I snuck in
your window.
The way you'd been sneaking
in and out,
afraid of the confrontation with the bail
bondsman,
me and my Xeroxed check,
another roommate's box of empty
chocolates.

On your bed, your clothes.
Your books, rummaged through.
Your dissertation, scattered on the floor,
and your climbing gear:
three different sized hexes,
two Camalots,
one gear sling
and an odd assortment of carabiners
left behind.

VI.
Skip,
the money you stole doesn't matter now.
I've found another climbing partner,
and I'm still holding your climbing gear.

At a University Poetry Reading

In the small makeshift auditorium,
       on the 3rd floor of the student
union   building, she's introduced by
her own words.
A term I don't understand but it's
supposed to convey a sense of how
precise, how talented, how much of a
better poet she is than the thirty of us
assembled in the fold-out chairs.

We could learn a lot from her,
       this reading, her first book, a
second to be published next year,
       and a third she's working on
called, "The Guardians,"
       but will probably be entitled
something else
       because she's probably not going
to include that poem (no one seems to
like it).

I admit I get lost every time she starts to
read, find my mind drifting to the corner
of the room and staring at the cobweb
silhouette projected on the back wall.

A couple of times she gets caught up in
her own words and I want to say, "Why

don't you just start over?" or "Maybe if you actually read that poem out loud before today, you'd know that that combination of consonants won't roll off your tongue as easily as it rolled out of your pen."

The things you notice when you look at a reading as a performance instead of as a lecture, workshop recitation, or dissertation defense.

When she talked about the killing of the polar bear that escaped from the zoo, and then "900 pounds of polar bear is a lot of polar bear,"

I wanted to leap from my seat and say, "You know, if you delivered that line just right, you could actually get a couple guffaws."

I'm not saying she's a bad writer and I'm not saying she's a bad reader because she was clear, didn't have too many annoying habits that distracted from the poems, but she left way too many things up to my imagination.

Why are poetry readings so damn serious?

What's wrong with engaging the
audience?
How much of the audience wasn't a
poet, a student of poetry, or somehow
affiliated with the English Department
that brought her here?

Is reading poems to poets somehow like
joining a country club where everyone
looks and thinks like you?
Where are all these non-poet people?
Cause they are certainly not here in the
small makeshift auditorium on the 3rd
floor of the student union building eating
white cake and drinking tea.

No one claps, which startles me,
        because this is art after all,
            and she's reading.

We're paying attention (or trying to),
        and there is absolutely no clue in
            her performance
        that now is when
        the poem is over.

A Place for My Stuff

-for George Carlin-

Every morning, while waiting
for my English muffin to toast,
I drink a glass of water and take
an inventory through my kitchen
window on how many people
stayed in the old church across
the street's abandoned parking
lot through the night? How
many are up at this hour: sitting
in the flowerbox asking for cigarettes,
making small talk (I suppose) with
the random dudes on BMX bikes
that seem to swoop in and out of
the parking lot at all hours? *"Too
many people pulled and pushed around/
Too many waiting for that lucky break."*

Yesterday afternoon, I noticed a cop
car with two cop bicycles stood up
next to it in the lot. Four cops
talked to the grey-haired black guy
next to the open rear door. He was
handcuffed, and it looked rather
routine. I watched (as I often do now)
as they gingerly directed him toward
the backseat. A few minutes later,
they shut the door and drove off.

The two bicycle cops folded up a
blanket,
pushed the scattered stuff onto an old
tarp
and placed it all together before
covering
it up with another tarp and left.

This morning, no one hung out in the
parking lot,
but this guy's stuff was still there.

The Haul

Visiting the new used bookstore, I'm surprised
to find *The Outlaw Bible of American Poetry*
prominently displayed for only six bucks.
Then find two baseball novels: *The Natural*

and *Summerland,* each two bucks.
After asking where the poetry section is
I glance through the two shelves
And then look up and see my book

on top of the shelf. I pick it up.
Their used price is six bucks. I open it;
the only inscription is a cursive, "read 8/11/13."
No signature, no dog-eared pages, or other writing.

So I buy it and think, "Hey I may not be
in the *Outlaw Bible*
But they thought my book was worth just as much."

Fences

Bent screws. Yard bricks displaced.
Wooden fence posts splintered.
A late night car hopped the curb,
ramped up my neighbor's driveway
and took out the corner of our fence.

A short fence, anyone could step
over it with almost no effort,
but it kept people out, kept
us safe random drunks, and
passers through that call
this part of the city home too.

I prune the mangled bush,
 pullout the corner post,
somehow broken where one
end met the Quickrete, and build
up the corner from those
displaced yard bricks and loose
soil so that the corner of our yard can
hold the fence upright once again.

A handful of new screws,
wood shimmied and screwed
in place, and the corner of our
yard looks about the same,
though now hiding some
rigged handiwork, to make

the fence upright and straight.

Repairing fences was not
what I thought I'd be doing
in this city life, but so it is
as I lock the door behind me
and sit to write this poem.

Almost Blue

for Chet Baker

I didn't even spot it until it moved
and it swept across my vision;
its wings a slow beating *whoop,whoop.*
Then it landed, across the shallow
channel
from the one time island
that lets me walk to the middle of the
Rio
without having to get my feet wet at all.
It stood and arched it's back
and its wings were grey, almost blue.

Almost blue.
Its color, and the noting it in my head,
and I thought of Chet Baker
his missing teeth,
and how I almost lost mine too
when drunk,
I wrecked my bike
and flipped over the handlebars
and met the pavement.
Bits of teeth now replaced by some sort
of dental cement.
I was more mad than sad,
more red than almost blue.

Almost blue.
The sky this morning is clearly blue

and the light plays tricks
as I can never really see the *Yerba
Mansa*
and it's green leaves turning red
as fall moves slowly down the *Rio.*
The *Great Blue Heron* stood erect,
peering at me and perhaps wondered as
I walked up towards him.
Am I a thing it should be bothered by
or is the sprightly, gangly black dog
that bounded in the water,
snapping at it to get its fill the real
threat?
The sky reflected in the muddy *Rio* is
almost blue.

Almost blue.
When I reached the tip of the island,
took a couple of pictures
it jumped up again,
whoop, whoop, whoop down the river
it's wings of almost blue beating the air
that lifts it up,
till it alighted on the southern tip
of my island.

Almost blue.
I know so little about Chet Baker,
only listen to his songs every now and
then,

but I wonder if he'd have traded his
heroin habit
to get his teeth back again.
My dentist wasn't particularly upset,
just asked if I'd worn my helmet (I
didn't),
and set to work on making my smile
look normal.
My white teeth, my red tongue,
and Elvis Costello's tune running
through my head
 Almost Blue.
Almost doing things we used to do
There's a girl here and she's almost you
Almost…

Poop on the Stoop

Always Thursdays, I work late.
So I schedule the bi-annual dentist
appointment,
and I'm out the door, on the trail,
soaking in the sunlight,
alone with thoughts
and finally heading back home,
before work,
when I get the call.
My wife's got a meeting and only has
time to water the garden before she
splits.
While watering the garden,
she noticed that the pansies had been
pulled out,
and a trail of toilet paper leads out our
yard to our front stoop.

"Someone has pooped
on our front stoop," she say,
"and I've got to go."
I want to feign off,
but it's my late morning and someone,
might as well be me,
has got to clean the poop
from our front stoop.

At home,
armed with hose, broom and dust pan,
I choke back bile
and clean our front stoop.
No more poop.
And yet, now I'm left with this,
this poem, the remnant of the poop on
our front stoop.

Got Rings

Still daylight and I'm just going
down the street, and some cat,
bag strapped over his shoulder
moves in and says, "Got rings!"

Now I'm not deaf, but my
hearing is going for sure
so I just ask, "Huh?" He points
to a finger, "Rings, real stuff."

Surely this isn't what he's selling
and he knows I know it, playing
dumb to hopefully skip away.
And I can't change my path,

or veer away too rapidly nor do
I want any. "Suboxone. Meth. Rings,"
he elaborates. And he's not walking
straight and could say I heard him

wrong or even just mumble
to the cops that might want
to know what he is doing
in the late afternoon behind

the University Church of Christ
and talking to some stranger

who is obviously passing through
and hoping to sell a ring or two.

Appellation

Say his name.

Say you've seen him walking down Central,
blending in with college kids, men who party early and often
and now, look at news stories, social media feeds and his arrest in Roosevelt Park
on a Friday afternoon.

Say fifteen years ago you and he were regulars in a dive bar on a regular week night
and you danced to a band that a lot of people found fun:
 an escape, path that didn't at all look familiar.

Say you'd talk on the patios, the bars that hadn't kicked him out
and you never knew his name.
Say his name.

Say you'd see him,
run into him at Walgreen's.

He'd ask you to buy him beer, hand you cash.
He'd lost his license and knew you as a familiar, friendly face.

Say you turned away and passed off the request, mumbling as you walked by.
He seemed a little bit lost, and you felt it just wasn't right,
like drinking wasn't also a way that you passed time.

Say you talked to your wife on what if anything you could do.
She worked in mental health, didn't have a quick fix but asked,
"Did he smell?"
No.
"Did his clothes look particularly ratty?"
Not anymore than usual.
"Did you acknowledge that you knew him?"
Sort of.

Say you'd seen him on Central by the University
and you knew he was "falling down."
You could see it but didn't know what else to do.

83

You'd bob your head in
acknowledgement as he walked by.

Say his name.
and read the article of his arrest,
indecent exposure to children in a park.
He'd been wandering around the park
and finally the police closed in after
someone took a photo.

Say he's more than a felon, a criminal,
mentally ill,
say we don't know how to help
sometimes,
and sometimes we're just afraid.

Say how else was this story going to
end.
Say his name.
Say his name.
Say his name.

Daily Special

*To the woman who works Central from University to
Maple*

As I fill her to go cup, I wonder,
Does she recognize me?
And as I give her the cup, I want to say,
"Are you okay?
Have you heard the blown rain on top of
rain fly,
the lazy sighing of Aspen and Pine in
the late May breeze,
the still, methodical rushing of river
water running down?
Have you seen the threesome of
chipmunks scurry over brush,
      loose volcanic tuft,
            and raven scat?
Have you seen the full moon streak the
cloudy sky
and watch the grey undefined cirrus
clouds move in
      and paint the sky a shade of
slate?
Have you heard birds or seen words
swooping overhead?"

And as she takes the cup from me, I
want to ask,
"Are you okay?

Because your mascara doesn't seem to
be coming together in the corner of your
eyes like I know you like it.
And the dirty Levi's that you wore just
the other day look a little bit more
scuffed
and slipping off your waist reveal a
crooked ladder of stretch marks
        and a second pair of exercise
pants underneath the dirty Levi's.
As you rub the rub the track marks on
your arm, your hands are shaking.
Fingernails bitten to the quick, wavering,
as you take the cup from me
        and you never
            smile."

Daughter, lover, sister, mother, friend,
life has yet to fill your cup, and all I can
give is ice.

The Yugoslavian

There are no pawn shops in Colorado City. That thought gives some solace to the rapid, albeit entertaining events that begin there when I pulled into a gas station on my way to Denver.

I was traveling to Denver solo because I was going to a funeral. Last minute, my partner couldn't get the time off and since she didn't really know my friend, here I was on the road, listening to music and deciding to stop for gas at the Diamond Shamrock because it was an easy exit off and on to I-25. It was a Thursday, the day before payday, and though I don't live paycheck to paycheck anymore, I don't generally keep a lot of money in checking account and the following day it'd fill back up: direct deposit. That thought also gives me some solace on the events that begin at the Diamond Shamrock in Colorado City.

I didn't see what direction he came from, but as I was taking the gas pump nozzle out of my tank a white Chevy Suburban pulled up behind me.

A man, mid 40's, bald leaned out the window and said, "Do you speak Spanish?" gesturing towards my New Mexico plates.

Thinking maybe he did speak Spanish I said, "Pequito."

With that he stepped out of the car. Walking towards me he said, "I'm Yugoslavian."

I nodded and put the nozzle back into the pump.

"We are on the way to Chicago and my card was denied."

I said, "Pull around I'll put some gas in your car."

He nodded. "No. I need money my friend."

I walked towards him and could peer into his car. In the passenger seat was a small brown-haired boy about eight years old. In the back seat was a woman, early 40s wearing a simple brown frock with her brown hair pulled into a bun and she was attending a toddler who was strapped into a car seat. The car was clean; the kids were clean and well-behaved; and the mother smiled up at me as I looked in. I said, "I don't have any money on me."

He didn't miss a beat. "They probably have an ATM inside."

I sputtered in agreement then said, "How much do you need?"

He was wearing two big gold rings and a gold crucifix attached to a gold chain around his neck. Both rings were on his right ring finger. He took the rings off. "These are 18 karat gold rings. I bought them for 3000 dollars."

"I definitely don't have that kind of money."

"If you could give me 300, I'd give you the rings."

"I'd have to see, but don't' think I have that kind of money."

"I'll give you this too," he said taking off his crucifix.

"Okay," I said. I started to walk towards the store, and he and his little boy followed me.

When we got to the store, I went to the right looking for an ATM and he went to the left. He found it and gestured towards me.

At the ATM, I checked my balance and showed him that I couldn't give him even 300. I said, "How bout 150?"

"No, no," he said, "Two hundred. Please."

I took out the money and gave it to him. As we walked out, he smiled and put his hand on my back. I looked at the two rings and chain and crucifix in my hand.   I handed him the crucifix back. "Here," I said, "You wanted 300."

His little boy was running towards the car. The woman was tending to the baby in the car seat, which was actually on the ground now between my car and theirs. She smiled too, and I watched them load back in and after a couple of minutes pull away.

I got back in my car and pulled around and before looking right, looked left to see their back plate. It was an Illinois plate, but I didn't really get a good look at it just really noted that it was white, like many of the Illinois plates that I'd seen.

Freddie the Freeloader

Let's get this story started
    'cause they kicked Freddie off
    the street
Told him he couldn't just hang
    around at these places where
    people meet

              Freddie couldn't sing
        But that didn't stop him trying…

Now Freddie looked up at me
    today, as I bent down
    and put a coin
    into his hat.
He said, "A bed," and then
    held his hands as if to pray,
    though my coin was far from
    doing that
              And then he started
                    singing…

I couldn't dig his song because he
    was just too much out of tune
Oh Freddie, you could be
    howling at the moon and it
    would still come out all wrong

and leave my ears a
ringing…

Even Freddie no longer bops
along like some
unacknowledged saint
to show me why I should
try to live
without complaint.

On a warming planet,
Freddie doesn't have
to be so cold
and reminds me what it's like
just simply growing old.

When you're listening to a tune
that really just sets you free,
remember they kicked Freddie
off the street,
and at the places where
people meet,
they told him he couldn't
beg for change
because change
might never come.

True Story

I don't often get a personal story to sort of reflect the reality of living in America. Everything seems so abstract, as happening out there, but this story sort of erupted into our lives on the second to last day of 2019.

First, some background: for the last 17 years, my wife worked at Albuquerque Healthcare for the Homeless, and I work at the community college, so we are both on the frontlines of what the lack of an adequate social safety net looks like. Most of the time, however, we can leave that behind at the end of the day.

For the last two weeks, I've been on holiday and living In the very comfortable confines of my sister's house in the mountains above Fort Collins. But upon returning to Albuquerque, the problem of homelessness came into a new stark relief.

Setting the context: The first time I noticed Hank, he was shuffling north to south then back again on the median of our street as it neared the busy intersection. He was older, about five-eight, had a short, ragged mess of gray hair, and a strong gravelly voice.

The next time it was because my dog bounded out of our front door and barked at him at the front gate.

Our stoop is shielded from the street by a juniper bush and a small crop of bamboo. On the stoop, one can stash belongings on the terrace behind the bamboo, and it isn't visible from the street. Hank had taken to putting a small grocery bag with clothes and a couple of books on the terrace and, when he wasn't shuffling on the median, sat there and read.
With our dog erupting at the gate, he stood up, apologized and started to walk away.

"It's okay," I said. "She's just super territorial. You can stay there if you want."

For the next week or so, I'd see him every other day, sometimes on the median, sometimes resting on our stoop reading. He'd get up when we left the house or shuffle off as we came home. He never entered the yard, nor talked to us very much.

My wife learned that his name was Hank and after checking in that he was okay asked if he knew about the various services around town.

He did.

I don't exactly remember, but I think at one point my wife offered some gloves or something, so, while the dog was erupting in the house, he came into the yard.

The sort of invisible barrier that kept him out of our yard and, mostly, on the periphery of our lives has been broken. But, for the most part, I was wrong.

With winter approaching, we didn't see him on our stoop much. He wasn't escaping the heat, and the next time I remember seeing him, he was sitting next to the smoke shop next door. He was huddled next to the entrance and looked really cold.

We had just gotten off the bus and were heading home. Once home, we grabbed an old pair of gloves and a really nice jacket that we'd gotten but was too big for her and too small for me. We went back to him and offered him both. He took the gloves but refused the jacket. He said his pea-coat was keeping him warm.

With the holidays, we were visiting family, so I'm not sure if he came by or checked in on us. I didn't notice him being around when we got back, but last night, our dog erupted after we'd gone to bed.

We live in a pretty busy neighborhood, so it's not uncommon for her to bark at people talking too loud as they walk by or people arguing in the empty parking lot across the street. Most of the time, I just come out and see what's up, and she'll settle down.

Sometimes I put on a long video of white noise to hide the background noise, and we can make it through the night.

Last night, however, was neither of those. As I looked out, I noticed Hank was actually banging on our screen door. I opened the door, trying to keep the dog away from it, but couldn't really understand what he was saying over the barking. Finally I said, "Hold on."

In the bedroom I said, "It's our friend."

My wife got up and got dressed. I got dressed, and we came back out to the living room. She opened the door as I held the dog, which seemed to calm the dog down.

"If I could just sleep on your floor?" he asked.

They talked some more, and she explained that even though it was really cold, there was no way he could stay here. We both understood that, and I, admittedly, was thankful our dog was so inhospitable. I said, "I know it's a slippery-slope, but we can't be his go-to guy."

Finally, she got him to let us take him to the emergency room.

Outside, he mentioned he'd lost his gloves. His hands were wrecked. Torn band-aids, chapped dry skin, and his fingers barely moved. It took both of us to get him to stand up, and we shuffled out to the car. He was barely able to stand, let alone walk.

In the car, he complained about making sure the heat was on and where it was blowing. Once it got going he held his hands in front of the vent. My wife and Hank disembarked at the emergency room entrance, and I went around to the parking garage. When I parked, I followed the maze of entrances and found the emergency room.

She was nowhere to be found. After about fifteen minutes she came back and said that she'd started to walk around the building but realized that I'd parked and entered in some other way.

We left Hank under the supervision of the emergency room. They were going to run some tests to make sure he was okay.

In the car, she remarked about the directness and lack of urgency that everyone in the hospital seemed to demonstrate. "They just don't seem to care."

I said, "I'm sure this happens all the time. I mean where else can people go?"

The Scofflaw

Two minor fender benders,
Two major wrecks,
Once being thrown through
a front window and waking up
in an ambulance I realized

I hate cars even when
the weather turns
and the wind blows
icicles into my fucking wet hair.

I hate dangerous, dangerous cars
because they blow by and honk then
pull up to the next curb right in front of
me;

I hate cars because they are driven
by people with nothing better to do….
than drive and eat dinner,
drive and put on make-up,
drive and drink coffee,
drive and pluck hair,
drive and put on DVDs,
drive and text.

I hate cars because car drivers kill
bikers. You do.

Not that I could prove it in court,
but humans were in such a hurry
that they compressed air
and gasoline in a combustible engine
then strapped it to a metal cage
with speakers so they could listen
to Limbaugh or NPR or bad music
at 50 miles an hour and they
all want to kill me.

They do; you do.
I'm the scofflaw cyclist riding
in the middle of the lane,
running red lights and four ways,
jumping the curb to the sidewalk,
crossing lawns and annoying your dog
wearing dark clothing, refusing to signal,
never surrendering the right of way
as I flip you the bird when you lay
on your horn.

You are oblivious and run red lights
while on your cell phone,
turn right but only look left,
speed up to 30 on a street posted as 18,
slam on brakes and reverse

into parking spaces without even
looking,
and swing your car door wide
open and right into me.

Bring it on, Oblivious!
I ain't making it easy for you.
I'm off the road as fast as I can be.
I'm wearing dark clothes.
I'm removing my reflectors.
I'm never signaling, never using a light
because if you see me, you'll hit me.
Give it your best shot, oblivious.

Just remember when the next Polar
Vortex comes and freezes the Northeast
like a sno-cone and all those obnoxious
New Yorkers pile in their "never been off
road" SUVS or mini-vans with DVD
players
and move to New Mexico,
I'll be the one biking by you in a traffic
jam
on the Paseo Del Norte parking lot
or Coors loading zone and getting
to work on time because I don't need
parking or gas or insurance.

So, face it Mr. SUV, Mini-van,
boom car, trucker, I'm the future
and this future is passing you by.

Damen Stop

A rickety ride
on the Blue Line to Bucktown.
Snow falling on the city as we grind up
the self-imposed hill
as the train goes from subway to
elevated
and the city opens up down below both
windows:
small wooden decks with neglected
grills,
graffiti only a commuter will see
and no eye contact,
headphones,
small quiet conversations,
people concentrating on books
as each stop is announced
and suddenly its Damen--my stop.

Platform made of steel,
covered in creaky weathered wood
with grey snow pushed up into corners
and the crowd steps off the train into
weather,
windy, wet, wintry weather
and we wind our way around an equal
number getting on
and we march in asyncopation,

bottled up behind a big, lumbering black
woman,
carrying too many bags to make these
slip-steel steps
something navigated haphazardly.
She slips...
and the air from the rush hour
commuters withdraw in one long,
uniform gasp.
No one,
no one steps around or over,
even people down below her stop and
crane their necks to check-in.
"Are you okay?"
comes a muted question from someone
on the Damen stairs.
She mumbles, then lumbers up,
with the help of some stranger as he
helps her down the steps.

Chicago...Carl Sandburg calls you the
"City of Big Shoulders,"
and today you showed me why.

The Day the War Began.

Three deep and two dozen across, the Albuquerque police department blocked eastbound Central Avenue. They wore Army fatigues, gas masks and helmets, held black batons, yet had no badges or name tags that identified each as a person, an individual. Judging from the surrounding army of police cars and police horses, and the four cruisers that closed Central farther to the East, their function was clear. Not only do the authorities want to silence dissent, but they want to keep those not politically vocal from becoming aware of dissent at all.

One of the cops held what looked like a toy water cannon and swung it back and forth across the crowd. The gun shook, and he looked over to his right and then his left as if waiting for the right provocation.

Behind me, in the westbound lane, the crowd dispersed, moving off the street and onto the sidewalk. Most of the protesters now lined Central. A few of them, too few, sat down in the street. They looked around, suddenly realizing the support that was there seconds ago had dispersed, leaving them a small half dozen against the line of police.

To my left, some sort of gas canister rolled into the crowd blocking the Frontier restaurant. With gas billowing from the canister, the crowd ran back away from the restaurant, into the street and onto the other side of Central. A protester, clutching a bandana over her mouth, picked up and rolled the canister back toward the line of police.

The rain began to fall.

I walked up to the now lone protester and leaned up to her and said, "You can get off the street."

She nodded, but stood there.

Suddenly, the nervous cop grabbed me and pulled me towards him then pushed to his right.

I didn't resist, but moved with him and found myself seeing the protest from his vantage point. The angry crowd yelled and chanted from the side of the street. Whoever had led the protest had either abdicated that responsibility now or become just another face in the mob. Chants of "Shame on you, shame on you," emanated from a smaller and smaller crowd. Cops were everywhere, lining Central, blocking off Cornell, barking orders from horseback and waiting. I moved over to the sidewalk and looked out onto the street.

She was standing alone in the middle of Central when he opened up with the gun. Armed with bean-bag pellets, the cop fired one after another into her body as she crumpled and fell. My eyes burned as I stepped out into the street. No one approached me or, from what I could tell, even noticed me as I walked across the street to where she was lying.

She writhed in pain as I bent down and asked, "I'm Don. Is anything broken?"

She shook her head "No."

"Can you stand up?"

She moved around and then, grabbing my arm for support, pulled herself up. We walked over to the corner, and she slumped under the stoplight.

I bent down with her. "We're in front of the Frontier now."

I glanced around and stared at the line of police. Blocking the entrance to the Frontier, a small female cop with blonde hair bleeding out from beneath the fatigues looked around at the other cops.

She could be my sister, I thought to myself. Having just graduated from the academy a year before, my little sister is a cop in Denver. Certainly she was doing this very same thing, or so I thought.

Protesters were yelling at the cops, indiscriminately. On the last rainy day of winter, the cops of the City of Albuquerque were an army, and neither of us knew what we were doing or what was going to happen next. The real authorities were on the other end of phone lines, talking to the cops on horseback or standing next to cars, trying to coordinate a situation that had gone horribly wrong. The citizens of Albuquerque were in a standoff with the cops of Albuquerque. Somebody's brother held a baton. Somebody's sister yelled, "Shame on you," and curled her hand into an accusing finger.

I leaned over to a screaming protester who I knew and said, "They're just doing what they're told. Heather! They just want us to go home. We've made our point."

But had we?

What I only partially realized last March is much clearer now. In my concern for the lives of innocent Iraqis, I'd taken to the street. And on the street, seeing the show of force by the Albuquerque police department, I'd lost track of the police's humanity. They became the man, a machine. And, judging by their reaction, I became a rioter, a possible looter, a criminal. I'm still opposed to the war but find myself

making excuses for not speaking out.
I'm afraid and effectively silenced.

Chain Reaction

This is how the deal goes down,
a not-so-subtle reminder of domino
hitting domino,
of butterfly wings stirring up gale force
winds,
of chlorofluorocarbons depleting ozone,
one molecule at a time.

At a protest, our voices become one
and drown the din of television, position,
tradition, and greed.
A man rolls by in a Saab,
rolls down his tinted window and gives
me the finger,
a woman yells, "Get the hell out of the
road!"
And I stare and parade to the center of
the road
to show her even though I don't own a
car,
I still own the road.
But pedestrians don't need roads.

Too many dominos have fallen.
Too many butterflies have flapped their
wings.
I am letting them place the dominos on
the line

and set the butterflies free.
I am at a decided disadvantage in a
game that's fixed.

Broken, I head for home and stop at
Burger King.
Too lazy to think ahead, their weaker
impulse preys on my weaker impulse;
their   greed preys on my laziness.
Like a fluorine molecule breaks away
from chlorine and carbon
preys on that spare oxygen in ozone,
strips ozone out of our atmosphere one
molecule at a time,
they prey on me.

While I'm eating my lazy meal,
a cop pulls over a low rider.
His 4 inside lights alternate with his 2
outside lights
in a pattern one can't help but notice:

                  INSIDE

OUTSIDE

                  INSIDE

                                    OUTSIDE

                 2 ORANGE

1 RED

                 2 ORANGE

                                   1 BLUE

                 2 ORANGE

1 RED

2 ORANGE

1 BLUE

In minutes, he's got the passenger
spread eagled against the car and he's
barking in his ear from behind.
Resting one hand on his shoulder
and kicking the back of his right leg
because....

Because homey is paying for my
laziness
and the cop is paying for corporate
greed.
I'm shoveling garbage down my throat
shoveling greed and hypocrisy down my
throat and having homey taken away for
the crime of riding in a car, burning fossil
fuels,
being the subject of this poem.

Who's the criminal?
Homey or the cop?
Corporate greed or human laziness?
CFCs or Ozone?
Butterflies flapping wings,
domino hitting domino.
Who's the criminal here?

The Walk Home

Downtown is not so far away as to
always necessitate driving,
so with tickets in hand we headed west.
Walking through our neighborhood until
it runs into the hospital
then a block north to go under the
interstate and, six blocks later,
the railroad tracks on Central Avenue,
Route 66.

Some of the storefronts are empty.
The buildings a bit dilapidated,
but for the most part the walk is
uneventful,
especially during daylight hours.

As we approach downtown
we have to navigate the underpass,
but after living here long enough,
we know its just keep our heads down
and our feet moving.
In a short time, we pop out just east of
the busy downtown district
and the historic theater where we are
seeing a touring band from Minnesota.

A couple hours later, without much
fanfare, we exit the theater after dark
thinking if we time it right, we just might
catch the bus back.

At the last stop before the underpass,
we realize by the time bus arrives, we'll
be mostly home, so, we cross to go
under the tracks.

Just before we start, a man, medium
build,
gray hair, says, "Great show, huh?"
We shake our head yeah, having not
even finished talking about it yet.

"Are you guys heading that way?" he
asks pointing to the dark underpass.
We nod.
He asks, "You mind if I walk with you?"
We say, "Sure."

As we walk, we learn he's from out of
town, a small Arizona town,
and came in to see the band from
Minnesota.

He's staying at the hotel just up the
road,
and Albuquerque freaks him out.

Packin'

for Philadelphia-- the City of Brotherly Love

Yeah, that's right.
I'm packing.
I am.

I'm packing my wallet, my keys, my
watch,
the card key to my hotel,
my PDA ,
and my journal with pen in case I get
inspired on the subway.

Yeah
and when I passed you on the Ben
Franklin bridge,
then stopped,
I was only checking out to see if I could
make out the hours for the Riverside
Rink,
lit up,
not thinking you would catch me.

You looked at me as I spun away to
follow you down the stairs to Columbus,
and you stopped after 3 steps
and looked at me as I passed you on
the left,
my engagement ring 'tinging on the rail.

I'm a guy,
so by definition, I'm a danger.
So, I don't blame you.
You're a woman,
reading a book as you walk across the
bridge,
but you're not sporting headphones,
and you're not afraid to make eye
contact with me
some 6 foot tall,
bulging layers'
long haired,
goatee sportin'
200 pounds of potential menace,
a nightmare that livin' in the city
told you to be on the look out for.

Yeah,
I'm packing
I'm packing a string of words
that I want to direct at you,
for assuming the worst:
Assuming I might sneak up,
throw your arm up high and twist,
reach around and slap my large hand
over your mouth to silence you
as I used my 200 pounds and dragged
you somewhere
anywhere that was dark, obscure, lightly
trafficked.
Cause I know that fear is healthy,

sometimes, and fear is what keeps you
safe, but I'm still a little shook up
because I'm afraid of the me you saw.
You saw me as some creepy, bearded,
overweight stranger, eyes perhaps a bit
too narrow, looking at you a bit too long,
hands clenched in fists, and not talking
on a phone or listening to an iPod.

I'd probably not want me following
myself either.
It's enough to make my mind spin in all
these different directions, that it wasn't
going to before this night.
Yet, I'm not too sure
I want my mind to go there, to think that
in an alternate universe instead of
thinking about being mugged beat
down,
harassed, I'm the mugger, junkie, rapist
assailant who women wait for, standing
on the third step, in the light.
so that I can pass and put these 36
steps between us on a busy street at
8:30 on the day after Valentine's day in
Philadelphia,
the city of brotherly love.

No Means No

She'd relented; the apartment number was 213; she'd be ready by seven. And now, seven had come and gone, and he stood on the small walk-up to her second floor apartment, and the door never opened. Just leave. She's not answering. The small thin door stood in the shadow of the building and seemed to bounce the sound back at him, reject him. Now all he could look forward to was the few CDs he'd brought and the hum of a well tuned engine, the drone of rubber on pavement, and the air through open windows. All alone. This was his not their trip now.

It felt possible a month before when he met her. She was young, just a few years out of high school and kept her long straight, dirty blonde hair pulled back into a ponytail. She had green eyes, and stood maybe five and a half feet tall. At the front host stand of the mid-size Mexican restaurant where he worked, she turned in her application to the host.

"Hold on. Let me see if the manager can talk to you now."

The host walked over to the open office door. "Do you have time to look at this?"

D. was sitting in the office, looking over an inventory list and staring up at an open cabinet. Rows of liquor bottles were lined up with the labels facing out. Each bottle behind the bottle in front matched exactly: the same make, brand, and label lined up like soldiers. "Hold on." D. marked something on a form then closed the cabinet, pocketing the keys after locking it. The office was a triangle inside the outside corner of the building.   Two built-in desks butted up against the inside wall and two sets of cabinets, which flanked a cold metal safe. Clipboards hung from hooks, pencils and pens, tickets thumb tacked to corkboards, and a note from the

General Manager that said, simply, "Do a liquor order." He took one step then took the application from the host's hand. Glancing at it quickly, he followed her out of the office.

M. was sitting on the small bench looking at the menu.

"You ever bus tables before?"

She looked up then answered, "Not really."

"You have any problems working Friday or Saturday nights?"

"No. I'm totally free."

"Great. Come back tomorrow at ten A.M. and I'll get you started."

"That's it?"

"Yep, that's it." He strode over and held out his hand. "I'll see you tomorrow. Just ask for D."

They shook hands and he spun around with her application in his hand

and went back into the office, shutting the door behind him.

M. stood in the lobby and looked out at the restaurant. Thursday morning and the restaurant had just opened. The tables to the left of the host stand were set but empty.   Morning light streamed through a skylight illuminating the light red and brown color motif. A wooden sculpture of a Native American pueblo stuck a few inches out on a wall that separated the seating area from the back of the house. There was an equal split between tables and booths, a couple of two-tops and a couple of six-tops. Another section was barely visible in the back of the restaurant. It wrapped around and joined the section hidden behind a swinging door to her right. Directly behind the host stand and a couple of steps up from the rest of the floor was a small bar; the beer cooler visible through a sliding door that opened opposite the manager's office. As she looked, a busser came up to the host stand, flipped open a small day timer on the host stand, and mumbled to the host, "Just one, huh." He was wearing a maroon polo shirt with the name of the restaurant, "Papa's Cocina" stitched over the left pocket, and black slacks.

"I was thinking tables forty five and forty four?"

"I'll get it ready now then."

M. spun away and left the lobby. The door slapped open and then closed behind her sounding like a single knock.

Papa's Cocina was a full service Mexican restaurant in the Northeast Heights. With the exception of the first year, D. had worked there since moving to Albuquerque. On the surface, it reminded him of working at Jose O'Reilly's in Boulder, Colorado, which admittedly was a good job (for restaurant work) that every place then got compared to, yet the comparison's seemed to arc back to Boulder, and Albuquerque would never be Boulder.

Not to put too much of a point on it, but Albuquerque could never be Boulder. Boulder held almost mythic status for him: tolerant, fun, stimulating, rich (he'd never noticed before). Strange how the trajectory of his life merely changed locations because in Boulder he was being groomed for management when he moved to Albuquerque with his girlfriend and, after a year of trying on different restaurants like he was trying on hats, got promoted to management at Papa's Cocina, which could never be Jose O'Reilly's. The differences were stark and significant, yet the biggest difference was the relationship between the management and the staff.

In Boulder, management and staff weren't as clearly demarcated. The General Manager and Kitchen Manager shared drinks with the staff at the end of a busy night, the assistants made arrangements to see concerts in Denver and take camping trips in the mountains. Relationships began; friends became roommates, and relationships ended. In

Papa's Cocina that was frowned upon; the management didn't fraternize with the employees, and the employees were encouraged by scheduling to keep this clearly a job. He was their boss, not their friend.

In Boulder, the management understood that almost everyone, even the management, was attending the university, so shifts were predictable: the same management worked with the same staff. Though being the location of the state school too, Albuquerque was not a college town, so outside of the neighborhoods surrounding the university, businesses didn't cater to the whims and demands of college students. And the owner liked the management staff to be nimble, at his beck and call.

When D. became a manager, it became clear rather quickly that establishing any sort of routine outside of work would not be tolerated; he was expected to work any shift, expected to call in on a regular basis to see how things were going, expected to change his schedule when cooks called in, bartenders didn't show up, or even wait tables when a big party made a reservation on short notice.

For a person who'd moved to Albuquerque just the year before, D. knew almost no one when he started managing.

This was not Boulder; the job was lonely, frustrating, and demanding. And D. would sit in the office and read the paper, not looking at the classifieds because, "every restaurant is going to be same," he'd said to his girlfriend when she gave him the recurring, "you can always just quit" or pore through the books he'd not gotten to in college: Jack Kerouac, Hunter S. Thompson, genre fiction. Outside of the restaurant, his life was largely imaginary.

And after a few years of this he was single, again. A little over a year ago, he and his girlfriend (after moving down here from Boulder several years before) parted ways. It was rough at first, but he'd gotten used to it: sort of.

When the day came for M. to start, D. hadn't even looked over the application.   Snap judgment and now, just an hour before her scheduled shift he noticed the string of jobs: two months here, a week there. What he liked was where she lived (the apartment complex next door) and her availability (no preference for days or nights). She was twenty-two and still listed her parents as her emergency contact. He called her and told her she'd just need to wear a pair of slacks (preferably black) and comfortable shoes.

At ten, she came into the office and quietly stood in the doorway while D. grabbed forms and a pen from the filing cabinet below the desk. She was cute, he'd noticed now, and pretty in that understated not call attention to herself way. "So, you're going to have to fill out a bunch of paperwork and then we'll get you going. You brought your driver's license and social security card right?"

"Yes sir."

"Please," he handed her the stack of papers and a pen, "call me D. You can sit down at the table in the next room. Can I get you something to drink?"

"No thanks."

Bussing tables, as he explained, was not rocket science. Bussers were assigned specific sections and areas to keep stocked up and clean. They navigated the requests from wait staff, customers, and host staff to make sure the customers were happy and the tables were cleaned and turned over in a timely fashion. M. picked it up fast and by lunch rush she could handle the whole restaurant without much effort displacing the regular busser who just hung at the front host stand and laughed and talked with D. and the host for the remainder of his shift.

At the end of the shift, D. gave M. a weekly schedule: a couple of days and a couple of nights and gave her the skinny on wanting specific nights off: "No promises, but I'm pretty understanding especially if you like music. You like music?"

During her first shift he talked to her about music. Traveling to Kansas City to see the Grateful Dead, shows at Red Rocks, bands that nearly made it, conversations with guitar players, doing too many drugs and drinking too much.

She'd laugh, occasionally remark "That's the music my parents listen to," then swoop away from him in a bustle of work: fill up the tostada chip warmer, stock glasses, clean tables, bring chips and salsa to another table. She kept her distance from the crew as well, not hanging out after her shift, or opening up much.

Meanwhile he was playing loose and fast with the policies: buying end of night drinks for the staff, letting food mistakes get consumed by the bussers, spending most of the slow nights talking with customers in the bar.   He'd been doing this too long and knew the owner's routine.

Two weeks into her tenure, he got a new job. He was tired of the drive and had been offered a job managing a coffee shop downtown. They met his salary demands, and he was starting at the end of August.   The time left was a blur, shifts went by uneventfully, interviews, inventory, end of night books, greeting customers. With just a week left he planned a trip to see his family before starting the new job.

"So, have you ever wanted to do something crazy?"

"Not really."

"Come on," he poked her shoulder. "Like something that would surprise everyone."

She was putting glasses up on the shelf, extending as she slid them back to the back of the shelf.

He stepped back and took her in, long hair, young, firm body. "No. Like just drop all responsibilities, stop paying rent, get rid of a lot of shit."

She stepped back down and flipped the rack off the shelf. "My last boyfriend did that and had to move in. Really annoying."

"I don't mean to be a slacker or a mooch. I mean, just take a break and not worry about things for a while."

"It'd be nice, but I've got bills to pay."

He was her boss, did her weekly schedule, assigned sections to her at the beginning of the night, and hired her. Tolerating him was just something that she did; everyone had to tolerate one manager or another, and it was clear that the managers had to tolerate the owner. Deception. Contempt. Power dynamics, the hierarchy bred this, created it. And the conversation went like this for a couple of days, him always bringing it up, just sort of dabbling in the idea and sort of dragging her into it. He felt like he just didn't have anything to lose. Though, she didn't know that.

"Why don't you come with me?"

"Excuse me."

He was talking to her in the break room.

"Haven't you ever wanted to do something really crazy?
Like just take off and not worry about the consequences?
I've got money and a car, you'd just have to bring clothes, and we could go."

"And do what?"

"We could go camping, hang out."

"But you barely know me?"

"I'm sure we'd get along fine. We get along now. Why would we not get along?"

She moved around him and went out into the restaurant.

Something felt off, and he knew it, but he'd latched onto an idea, a crazy idea and now just ran with it. Most everybody knew he was leaving in a week and just going through the motions of managing anymore, hanging out with the regulars in the bar longer than usual, meeting the staff for drinks after shifts, and getting out all this bottled up energy that needed to get out. Was he deliberately sabotaging his ability to get hired back? He'd already come back once and that had been a mistake, yet, sometimes the devil that you know....

For the next few days he continued to badger her, suggesting they hang out after work, talk about what they could do if they went away, and she responded, but only in the vaguest of ways. Finally, just a day before he was scheduled to leave she said, "Okay. I'll do it. I'll go with you."

He was floored. If this was a bluff, she'd called it. Something about the whole exchange thrilled him, reminded him of the crazy things that Kerouac or Thompson would do. He even pretended that the trip could be platonic when that was clearly not what he wanted.

Now, he was standing at her door and knocking. No answer. The place was dark and the blinds were closed. There was no movement on the other side as he knocked.   She'd relented. She said she'd be ready, and she wasn't. The small thin door stood in the shadow of the building and seemed to bounce the sound back at him, reject him. Now all he could look forward to was the few CDs he'd brought and the hum of a well-tuned engine, the drone of rubber on pavement, and the air through open windows. All alone. This was his not their trip now.

He walked down the stairs looking at his full car in the parking spot. He had camping gear, two different brands of beer, a bottle of whiskey, a couple of joints, a bag of grass, and a quarter ounce of mushrooms. On the seat next to him was a small notebook and pen. He didn't want to be alone, but what choice did he have.   Opening a beer, he pulled out of the driveway. It was eight in the morning, but what did it matter; this was vacation.

Two weeks later he was back in town. He'd been reluctant to call anyone from the restaurant, but they had called him. On the message, they wondered if he knew what happened with M. He called, and they told him she'd never come back to work and didn't pick up her last check.

"She's disappeared." One of the cooks who lived in the same complex hadn't seen her.

"One of the servers said she was going with you on your trip."

"That was the plan, but I don't think she wanted to go."

"So, why do you think she said she would?"

He held the phone away from his ear for second. "I don't think I gave her much choice. She couldn't figure out any more ways to say, "No," and I wasn't listening."

Nevertheless, he ended up coming back to Papa's Cocina one last time after he flamed out at the coffee shop. The new management would only let him cook.

Even then he could only handle that for a few months before he moved on and found a waiting job at a place closer to downtown.

A Supermarket in Albuquerque

"What thoughts I have of you" today,
Allen Ginsberg,
as I navigate the crowded aisles of the
grocery store
on the day before Thanksgiving.

In my last-minute errands before I slip
into the holidays,
I thought this had the makings
of a poem, then thought that you had
already written
that poem, and my poem, however well-
intentioned
or, hopefully, well-crafted, would simply
be derivative.

I swerve past the bread aisle, my usual
first stop,
then realize my choices were being
made for me by the dinner invite, the
confirmed
recipes and just ignored the mountain
of meat, packages of pork and poultry
under the bright
lights before I stopped to let another
cart by in front of the meat counter

137

and then finally stopped in front
of the light green of the stalks
holding up the flowered broccoli.

No, it is the organic broccoli
with their smaller stalks that I am looking
for and the dark green of kale
that my wife slipped on to my list
as I never eat the stuff.

But then, a few aisles over, I stand
frozen,
wondering if Sweet Potato Pie could be
made with Yam.
Instead, I opt for the Stokes Purple
Sweet Potato thinking just because the
final
product would no doubt look more royal
purple than burnt orange,
it would probably still taste the same.

There, hovering over the cheeses
is our friends who we will break
bread with tomorrow in lieu of traveling
out of state.
We joke and confirm
our recipes, hug, and mumble
an awkward "Good-bye."

The bottleneck at the dairy section

causes another pause as I ask the
stocker
if there are any pie crusts
or had I just missed the section.
He looks up and simply says, "We're
out"
and goes back to stocking yogurts.

"Where are we going," Allen Ginsberg?
As another thing on my list is missing
and I realize I will have to navigate
another store or might not be able to
make the pie at all.

I think of you Allen Ginsberg
and the throng of faculty members
that surrounded you when I heard
you read at the auditorium
from my days in college.

You, in professing love for young
men would, no doubt, be called
out and have to deal with the
repercussions
of power imbalances, asking for
consent,
and yet, you died before
any of that could tarnish your reputation.

"Ah dear father, graybeard,

lonely old courage teacher,
what America did you have"
when you died from complications
of liver disease brought on by hepatitis
in 1997.

Do you think death has no use for an
afterlife,
does not allow an overview observation
of poets
navigating the crowded aisles in
supermarkets
all wearing cautionary real-time masks
so that I can just keep my head down
and not acknowledge at least two other
poets I see in the store today?

Eat At Home

-for Olivia Gatwood and Tom Willis-

Another evening out, to-go meal,
boxed lunch, or last-minute
purchase of food,
my wife asks, "Why don't you eat at
home?"

Because eating at home
makes me forget the early
mornings, late nights,
damaged waitresses,
drunk managers, bosses
who looked down over
eyeglasses and then
expected me to sit down
with them and their wives
over dinner.

Because eating at
home doesn't stop
the dreams about
restaurant kitchens,
fast food shake
machines, and
contraptions that slice
tomatoes with merely
a push.

Because heating element
plate warmers melt cheese
on full plates that I pulled
from the "sky" with callused
hands.

Because my
skin remembers
the splash of hot
sauces, water
dropped in hot
oil. steamer
cabinets
hissing,
opening like a
safe.

Because grease coats my
clothes and shoes as I
scramble for change in my
sash.

Because I still dream about not getting
to my tables in time, not filling that iced
tea fast enough, not putting in that side
for sour cream or noting that that burger
should be rare or well done.

Because of conversations
with bar regulars who come
here for fun while I pour a
rum and coke, a gin and
tonic, a screwdriver and
wonder how they got out of
work so early, so early
every day.

Because my morning prep
cook dealt pot out the
back, and my evening
cook thought it would be
"cool" to dose the other
boss.

Because of one cook's
broken collar bone, another
bartender's ruptured knee,
my awkward firing of a
waitress who brought a gun
to my bar and showed it to
me.

Because of one regular's 86ing after
putting a hole in my wall and
then the quiet reflection as I
read the daily paper and saw

he'd been killed in a standoff
with APD the next day.

Because my day bartender
lay naked in his room after a
death dealing aneurysm for
two days before they found
him.

Because my night bartender
was hospitalized after
shooting up, getting his arm
infected, and visibly shook
from withdrawals when I saw
him in the hospital.

Because my feet hurt even
now and I don't want to stand
behind a counter, in a dish
pit, on the line, behind the
bar, at the host stand, on the
floor, and crunch numbers at
the end of the night to make
sure it all adds up.

Because the last
restaurant job that I
had was waiting
tables where the

owner broke down
how many
milkshakes I sold
as his wife pulled
up in a new SUV.

Because I worked in
restaurants for 20 years in
every position at every
conceivable type. Two decades
of learning how to cook, of
watching my specials become
menu items, my drinks get
highlighted and sold, my
policies and management style
leaving me with being many
people's first "good" boss.

Because the hospitality
business
to the people who work
there.

Because I want to leave a
generous tip, always, and look
the other way when you forgot
my side dish or overcooked my
burger

Because I want to say that I see you,
I hear you and know how hard this job
can be.

I don't eat at home
because our kitchen is
too small and my
imagination is too big.
I don't eat at home
because I want to be on
the other side of it for a
while.

I want to be a customer, a
regular, some patron
everyone is glad to see.

A Pistol or a Bottle of Perfume

for Randy Libby

She stumbles in, sits down, tears the
sunglasses from her bruised and
battered eyes,
and mumbles, "I am still with him."
He parades in, puts a paint flecked
cellular
on the table top and smiles.

"Do you want a drink?"
A power struggle-he knows I know his
usual-
a Jack and Coke and she a Margarita,
yet I make him say it anyway
as he lunges for his ringing phone
as if it was a pistol
or a bottle of perfume.

While talking on the payphone, he puts
his fist into my wall,
then clutches his last drink at my bar,
and wonders why
I am '86ing him.
And I want to clutch his hand
show him the hole in my wall
grab the still warm handset
and say,

"You can't take your frustrations out on me,
your girlfriend,
my wall,
your last drink
in my bar.
My drink is not a pistol
or a bottle of perfume."

His life hangs on a pistol,
with which,
behind the curtained window,
he can keep the cops at bay.
His life hangs on a bottle of perfume
with which,
behind the curtained window,
he clutches and announces,
"I have got a gun-and I will use it."

And who would the cops believe?
Him and their buddy behind the field
glasses
who says he is clutching something—
and it could just be a pistol
or a bottle of perfume
as his bruised and battered girlfriend
pleads,
"He doesn't have a gun."

They shoot him down,
behind the curtained window.

And he dies,
clutching a bottle of perfume
as if it were a pistol,
or maybe that last drink.

Superheroes

I don't usually title poems before I write
them, but as I was waiting for the
mandatory
fifteen minutes from getting a
vaccination
to leaving, I thought of superheroes.

As a kid, I collected comic books, but
didn't
know that they were valuable, so when
I shuffled off to a plane to live with my
aunt
and uncle while my parents wrapped
things up before joining us in another
new city, I had a small stack of comic
books I left behind.

The few I do remember, I eventually
replaced:
Peter Parker, the Spectacular Spider-
Man, number 10 and a run of issues
where the Avengers fought Graviton,
which was the only story that left me
hanging for years until I found it.
Graviton is really bettering the
Avengers, and when he goes to brag to
his love, Judy, she's nowhere to be

found.
He looks for her. He traces her steps
to the edge of the sky island where
they've been battling and she,
presumably,
jumped off. Heartbroken, he loses
control
of his power and then is beaten by the
Avengers.
Yet Judy didn't die; she was rescued
by Jarvis, the Avengers' butler at the
end.

Now my fifteen minutes is up, and I
snake
my way through the ever-lengthening
line
to my car and the traffic changing to
rush hour.
Doctors, nurses, scientists aren't battling
Graviton or rescuing a falling damsel in
a flying car, and they're not sandwiched
between newsprint ads in young boys'
imaginations.
Sometimes just filling out paperwork,
swabbing your arm and injecting a
vaccine, so that you can go home for
the holidays and not get your family sick
is all the heroism I need.

The Day I Wore a Dress

(I almost want to start this poem by
repeating the title,
but merely typing the above, I know that,
now, I don't have to).

Language has a way of creating,
so here I am...trying to tell you I wore
light brown loafers,
      red knee-high socks,
        a brown rayon dress
          with white polka dots,
        a simple, yet
          elegant necklace,
a pair of light blue sunglasses,
and a scarf.
Marilyn Monroe incognito.

(I'd like to begin to tell you about getting
up on a stage dressed like this, but
something else was happening.)

I bike.

All the cars at the first block let me go...
just another beard dressed up in drag.
Nothing new to see here, move along.

I merged on Lead and took the bike lane
down the hill, legs pumping like they do.
Cars slowed, stared at me, and I felt
watched.
An early Sunday afternoon.
I sat in the lane,
          lights flashing,
                    legs pumping,

wobbling to my left so I take up space
          that clearly belongs to me
                as the overpass reared up.
A Drag sandwich between concrete and
moving cars.

(I'd like to point out that I'm reading this
right now, so don't worry about whether I
make it or not. You can assume,
because I am reading, that I am not
another statistic,
another "accident" in a city built for
cars.)

But the dress wasn't helping much.
I was trying to be visible,
when a big part of biking in this town
is trying not to be visible but still being
seen.

Being alone and isolated isn't new.

Being vulnerable and in peril isn't
something that someone invites.
Yet, for a few minutes,
the sensation was far from pleasant,
and I had a choice.
I chose to wear a dress.
When we teach tolerance,
            we're trying to create a world
            where out of the ordinary is
            basically the way it is
A man can wear a dress.
A woman a rough cut of blue jeans;

But when I stepped outside,
(outside of what people expect to see),
I felt more than shame,
I felt alone, vulnerable, as if at any
moment I could be the subject of
someone else's poem,
instead of the one creating it.

Transfiguration

-for S. Dirk Anderson-

Contemplating our own deaths
we drove to the variety
of graveyards in the suburbs
west of Denver and walked
them while we smoked cheap cigars.

Always late at night,
we had no fear that we'd be
escorted out or forced to jump
a fence to navigate an escape.
We grew up, and never
repeated the exercise in new
towns, and traded cigars
for themed parties with cheap beer.

Graveyards now seem foreign.
Just visiting them now is like
an exercise in visiting a friend
in a hospital. It's not how we
choose to spend our time.
But then, again, neither
one of us has the time we had back
then: him, his wife, and two kids
and me, my wife, and ever restless dog.

The messages we exchange
now are shorter, sharing

necessary information, which friend
from high school has passed
on, and how our immediate
family is holding up.

If you'd asked me then if
we'd still be friends some forty
years later, I'd have doubted it
as I only understood time as etched
in stones with names I didn't recognize.

I recognize more etched names
now, but we still don't contemplate
death much as if it is just a turn
we'll make on a long road trip
with the fading center stripe
and mileage markers providing
the only guardrails to the actual
road we're taking.

We've both navigated the twists
and turns by not veering too far
to the left or right, but we feel
uncomfortable in the center too.
The adulthood that we seemed
so eager to get to wasn't all that
it was cracked up to be. Even during
the best of times It seems to be
just a series of things we have
to do each day and nothing more.

No time for contemplation; no desire
for it to make much sense;
no. it just goes on.

The Pass

At the northern terminus of Union Road, the suburb of Lakewood is split by the 6th Avenue freeway. To the north of the on-ramp is Simms road and a remote, lightly populated area of Lakewood dominated by Simm's Landing (a fish restaurant carved into the side of the hill for the view) with a sprawling three-tiered parking lot. Other easy-on, easy-off businesses line up on the frontage road as the 6th Avenue freeway pours under the Union Street overpass, which marks the point where Simms becomes Union. To the south of the on-ramp is Union and the area, still Lakewood, but called Green Mountain.

Each morning cars spill down Union from Green Mountain and pour on to 6th Avenue for the morning rush to downtown Denver as easy as water spills out of an upturned bottle with the lid off. It's the path of least resistance and the major way that people from Green Mountain get to work. So, obviously, the area around Union and 6th is a bustling commercial zone with restaurants, gas stations, and even the occasional bank and doctor's office to make it complete.

The freeway cuts Lakewood in half making Green Mountain feel like it is its own town with its fair share of traffic and congestion.

On Friday the commuters become revelers and spill into every bar lining Union, close enough to home to make Happy Hour pretty much a safe bet and far enough from work to be home. Union is lined with chain restaurants and bars, fast food joints, and then Chad's Union Street Cafe huddled below the Black Angus and next to the towering monolith of Jose O'Shea's. Serving standard bar fare, Chad's was local, or tried to be, and it was clear on a Friday afternoon that almost everyone made this a usual thing. Or that was what it looked like to me.

Having turned twenty-one at college in the fall, Chad's was not my hangout. The Lakewood I grew up in was not the Lakewood of the evening commuter. When I lived here, I'd been a kid and mostly hung out in parking lots and city parks, sneaking beers in the backs of cars as I made out with girls and had to settle for a hickey or a hand-job every now and then.

But I was home for the summer, and all grown up. So, Chad's was where I went. I was a college male home from school and thus I felt like this place was just too small and just not as cool as the places we hung out in Boulder. The music wasn't cool; the people weren't cool; the food was just passable; the politics was Reagan, and I knew what was going on and how much of a suburb Lakewood really was. At the time, I felt like I owned the town and could do as I please. It didn't strike me as strange to strike up conversations at every table. Though I'd been shy and withdrawn in high school, I knew many of the regular patrons by name even though they didn't remember me. But B. wouldn't be here for a while so I might as well make the best of it.

At a table, next to a post, T. and his brother chatted up two women I didn't know. T. was a neighbor from a house we moved out of my junior year. We'd played basketball every day and were close then, but after I moved away the relationship just devolved into the kind of relationship where we just cut each other down rather than let the other in.

"So, home from school?" he slurred.

"Yeah, thought I'd see what this place was like as I never came here before."

He had Cerebral Palsy, so trying to figure out if he'd had too much to drink was not impossible, but definitely hard. He sounded drunk and wobbled as he walked all the time. About the only way to really tell was his volume. "Are you going to work at Burger King again?" he yelled.

It was the truth and a dig, and I nodded my head as I slung back another swallow to hide my embarrassment.

There wasn't a lot of options, but it still seemed juvenile to work at the same place where I'd cut my employment teeth. I was in my third year of college after all, not some high school sophomore. But Burger King was flexible, and now paid enough to keep me going. Besides I knew the job. It would take a couple of weeks of reacclimating before I started hanging out with the Burger King crew, and when we did it was at Chad's or darting up the road on Wednesday to Black Angus for "Two Dollar Call It." In a way it was our own suburban version of the roaring twenties, we'd drink too much and no one seemed to care. We'd wind up throwing up in parking lots or out of passenger doors then laugh about it the next day as we started doing it all over again. Occasionally we'd drive into Denver, and I never remember driving back.

But Chad's was the hang out. The Happy Hour, just sit and talk kind of place that D. (the only friend I knew in all contexts-from high school to Burger King, to the University) hung out at all the time. Even though he lived in Boulder, he'd come down every other weekend or so to see his parents and then hang with me and B. at Chad's.

B. was a relatively new addition to the Burger King crowd. He was a few years older and sported an early Beatles' mop-top haircut and a really bad set of teeth. I never knew why. B. had a full throated, head tilted, from the diaphragm laugh, and it came quick, unrehearsed, and generously. He seemed to have experienced a world I was just beginning to understand. A guitar player, he'd toured with a reggae/funk band around the West, and always had a crazy story to tell about "almost making it."

And he had. He'd recorded a couple of albums with a reggae singer who'd I'd seen in Boulder. The singer had become a one-man band, playing the upper strings on his Martin for the bass line, then strumming the melody on the lower four. He'd set up a percussion box on the floor and played the bass drum with one foot on the mic'ed box and a tambourine with the other. It was a surprisingly full sound.

I don't know how long he'd been managing at Burger King when I met him that summer, but we clicked. He pretty much let me be, knowing I was only there for a short summer burst, and I listened to his stories with genuine interest. There wasn't too many people who interested me much at Burger King.

Though I still called them friends, college was doing what it did for a lot of people: broadening my horizons and thus hanging out with this new crew, which was really the old crew, didn't seem as much fun as before. They hadn't read the books I had, talked with the people I had, and hadn't attended the various lectures and events that now made Lakewood seem basically quaint.

I wished I'd been more understanding, but I wasn't. So, when D. was not in town, I hung out with B. at Chad's. We laughed and talked about the various shows we'd seen. In Boulder, I'd become a regular barfly and spent my time listening to live music at the various places scattered on the Hill or huddled around Pearl Street Mall. He knew the venues, and we'd trade stories: mine were about drinking a bit too much and falling in the creek, or wrecking my bike, or running into various band members in the bathroom and getting the run down. And B.'s, though not at first, were all about people not being what they seemed.

He never did talk bad about the reggae singer he'd played with before, but there was a sense of loss, like something had happened.

"No, no, we were great. We had a

great chemistry and he'd ask me to play a lick or dial it back and we would. On our last album, I even convinced him to slow down "Buffalo Soldiers," so it had this slow dirgelike quality, but done with reggae rhythms. He still plays it that way."

"So what happened then? Why did you break up?"

"We didn't really break up. He has a family and I don't think he really wanted to make the jump. It would mean going on the road more or moving. As a solo act he can make a decent income in the bars around Denver without having to leave his family. The next step would be touring bigger cities and though we could all be making it then, I don't think he saw that as a big enough payoff. The sacrifices would be too demanding, so he wanted to take time to re-group. We're still re-grouping I guess as he's never called me one way or the other. I could play with someone else, but I really don't want to start all over again."

"So Burger King?"

"Sure. It's not a bad job and the

hours are chill.   Being on the road is hard."

The night moved on and B.'s stories grew more elaborate and exaggerated: near misses with famous musicians, and multiple different versions of seeing the Beatles at Shea Stadium. B. was funny, doled his enthusiastic laugh with ease, and generous, buying drinks longer after my wallet had shrunk from modest to empty.

And I was drunk. Not a new feeling, but B. was the first to express any sort of concern. "Why don't you leave your car here?"

"How am I supposed to get home?"

"Don't. You can stay at my place. I have a couch and I'm just around the corner. Besides I have some more beer at the house."

I really was more messed up than usual and didn't relish driving up the hill, pulling into my driveway or possibly having to explain to my mom what I was thinking. It was a conversation we'd managed to not have for most of the summer, but it hung there at the back of my mind with every beer. I knew I wasn't supposed to drink and drive but did it too often and got away with it too much.

"Let me call the folks and let them know I won't be in tonight." It was still early so I went to the pay phone in the lobby and dialed the number.

She gave her usual consent and thanks for calling and I was on my way. She'd stopped asking about the quality of the accommodations or how I knew the person I was staying with a few years ago; we'd reached an uneasy truce with me finally getting that the priority was that I not drive drunk. I really didn't know B. all that well, but crashing on couches was not a unusual occurrence; parties often devolved into drunken slumber parties with multiple people passing out and waking up at all hours of the morning and sneaking out.

B. ordered some water, and we sat largely in silence as we watched the waitresses clean up tables, collect tips, and joke with themselves.

At his house, we snuck down a

side stairway into the basement. It was three rooms, with the kitchen a corner of the living room. Rock and roll posters adorned the wall, a shelf filled with albums sat opposite a small loveseat, and big bong stood sentinel on the coffee table. The loveseat faced a stereo, and the only television was a small one that was on the kitchen counter behind us. Next to the stereo was an acoustic guitar and a black case. A thin layer of dust gathered on the guitar.

We sat down on the couch and he talked about why he had certain posters up and not others: *Wish You Were Here,* the Beatles, handbills from shows all over Colorado, and over the stereo a framed collection of concert ticket stubs. He pulled a joint out of a pack of cigarettes that was sitting on the coffee table. "You want some?"

"Sure."

We smoked in silence. The pot (mixed with alcohol) worked its way through my system and I felt a general sluggishness wash over me like thin layer of film. My focus shifted, and I kicked off my shoes. He looked at the shoes then at me.

"I'll get you a blanket."

A few minutes later he tossed me a blanket. "You want me to get the light switch?"

"No. I can get it."

"You mind if I put on some Floyd? It's nice to sleep to."

"Sure."

He smoked another joint and about halfway through "Shine on You Crazy Diamond," he got up and went into the bedroom. I spread out on the loveseat without even turning off the light.

"Come in here dear boy/Have a cigar…" drifted out from the stereo and I woke up. Though I was pretty out of it, I woke up enough to hear some noises. I looked over to Billy's bedroom.

He came out of the bedroom and stood in the kitchen. He was naked and noticed I was awake. "You know I have plenty of room in the bed. You sure you don't want to sleep in there," pointing to the bedroom.

"Thanks, but I'll be fine."

"You sure?"

I nodded.

"Okay. If you change your mind, just come on in."

I didn't change my mind, and in the morning B. and I drank coffee and talked about everything but the awkwardness of the night before.

After I'd gone back to Boulder, he finally told me that he was gay. I nodded in understanding, holding my face expression free, and putting the pieces together of our interactions that summer. We'd stay friends for most of the next year and he'd come up and get drunk with us. Drunk, he'd hit on us making an argument that we should broaden our horizons, try it and see if we liked it. It became a sort of joke every weekend: who's B. going to hit on this weekend. Yet he kept coming back until we just stopped calling. I didn't go back to Lakewood the next summer and now called Boulder home.

Cinder Block

I'm on probation,
and the only way I get off
is if I find eight cinder blocks
to replace them-there milk crates
that my horniness has caused to crack.

And I get off probation,
     until I reinforce her bed
          before we break it.
So, with no money to my name,
I makes a few phone calls
     and finds eight cinder blocks
          and calls my friend and explains my
situation and asks that he drive across
town,
          picks up the garage door opener,
               drives back across town,
               opens the garage,
picks up the eight cinder blocks
and drives 'em down to her house,
so I can reinforce the bed
          and pull out them-there milk crates
               and see what I can do to crack
                    those cinder blocks.

Because I want to crack the cinder
blocks, them-there milk crates weren't
     enough.

And if she switched to box springs,
I'd want to compress every spring
    and break the box springs too.
And if she switched to a waterbed,
I'd want to stir up quite a tidal wave until
she'd be replacing that bed too.
And if she switched to floor,
I'd want to work so hard we'd register on
some Richter Scale
    causing warning sirens to go off,
        people to be runnin' away from
            windows
                and holdin' on to plumbing
                fixtures

If I could break every type of bedding
the way that we broke them-there milk
crates
then I'd be doin' it again,
and again,
and again.

That is, my friend,
how much I enjoy doing it with her.

Rebels

The slightly taller than me soda
    machine had a glass door that you
could
        open, but to unlock the clear glass
        bottles of Coke, made with real
          sugar, from their Individual slot,
            you'd have to insert a quarter
          to pull them free.

You could only pull one bottle free,
and, once freed, the release mechanism
would lock back up until another quarter
was inserted.

They weren't twist-off so you had to use
the metal bottle opener attached to the
side of the machine.

Even in my youth, this machine,
holding sentry at a filling station
outside the first of two bays at an old
mechanic's shop seemed way past its
prime, but it worked and the Coke was
cold
and for a summer, way underpriced.

So underpriced that it was worth it to
walk

the two miles to be able to drink a
couple bottles worth.

We'd walk up back streets and across
busy
intersections and would drink
our first bottles standing next to the
entrance as if we were early teenage
roughs from another bygone era with
leather jackets, which we didn't have,
and slicked back hair, which we didn't
do, but we knew the image we were
supposed to be
standing next to this soda machine
with just another quarter burning a hole
in our faded jean pockets.

The Choice

East Colfax is as close to the clinic as I
can get now, as if it is just a section of
town or paved over, converted to lofts,
transformed into a strip mall in the ways
that everything
eventually becomes lofts or strip malls.
It might still be there, which is to say that
I don't remember where it was.

I do remember her name, Dana, and my
relationship to her.
She was the girlfriend of my boss,
  also a quarter of our bowling team
  (a summer-time adventure I 've
never done since).
  She and he were in love and
would later fall into marriage
  and then, after a couple of years,
an unsurprising divorce.

I willingly volunteered for the task as
Dana pulled me over and explained that
she was pregnant and wasn't ready.

  He couldn't get off work (which at
the time made sense, but now…), so I
drove her from Lakewood (West Colfax
if you must know) to the clinic.

She needed someone to drive her to
and fro, someone who wouldn't question
what she was doing. It was her choice,
yet that choice is never made in a
vacuum
especially if the only clinic is across
town
and requires some other person to
choose to drive,

It's her choice, and he couldn't come so
I'd give up my afternoon to drive her
there and, as a stand-in, would act like
the diligent boyfriend in the waiting room
of the clinic.

My role had been cast as the quiet,
respectful friend, who'd perform his
duties but never bother them or ask
why. So, in the waiting room, I sat with
the mothers and crying girls and
determined women who waited their
turn.

Dana and I didn't talk, but eventually
she was called and disappeared behind
a beige door. Twenty minutes later she
re-emerged
and stood in front of me and said,
"That's it."

And that was it, I thought, until she sat down in the passenger seat and let out a long sigh.

"I couldn't do it," she said.

"But…"

"I know. I'll let him know."

There was no follow-up with her or him.

Forty years later, after their son growing up and moving on, I asked him if he remembers it. He says,

"Dana never told me about this."

"You didn't know?"

"No. I would've argued against it if I did."

Urban Planning

-after Wallace Stevens-

A white soccer ball bounced
off the curb and rolled out
into a busy intersection. No one
retrieved it, and for the rest
of the day it sat in the middle
of the intersection as the cars
chose to detour around
that block completely. No one
knows why, but soon people
were walking down the street
instead of driving. A hot dog
cart appeared one day and
the vendor started hawking hot
dogs, "Chicago style:" relish,
mustard, two tomato slices,
and a very purple chopped onion.

Every day from 11 am to 2 pm,
a DJ set up his turntables
and started spinning, and then
back from 8 pm to 11 pm. In any
kind of weather, he spun, setting up
at first a canopy, and then, eventually
a gazebo with portable propane heaters,
small lamps, and a couple wicker chairs.

In time, the soccer ball lost air

and was replaced, mysteriously,
by another soccer ball, still
in the box, in the exact spot
on what used to be the busiest
street in town.

The Mighty Mule

Because the bus turns left on Academy
and disappears,
I imagine the driver runs into Wild Oats,
     fills up with "Organic Sumatra,"
     pisses in the auto-flush toilet next
to the "Baby Changing Station,"
     runs back outside,
     straps in behind the wheel,
     as they spin the lug nuts with that
high compression drill
     that they set up at the
"Wild Oats/Nascar Lube & Brake
Express."
"Squeak, Vuvvvvv-Ummmp."
The double doors open before me.

Because all they do is drive around in
circles,
I imagine that driving a bus is akin to
driving in the Indy – only slower –
and since you can't talk to the driver and
must stand behind the yellow line,
driving a bus would be ideal for people
with short fuses and missing vocal
chords.
Thus,

winding down at the end of the day must
be a veritable symphony of hand
gestures, monosyllables and expletives,
As they describe their day of senior
citizens showing them pictures of their
grandkids
     as three legs of their walker creep
just inches over that yellow line
     in a revolutionary flaunting of
casual disregard for rules and
regulations.

Because Del Norte freshmen wait north
of Montgomery and the "upper"
classmen south, I bet a bizarre hazing
ritual in the hallway ensues,
     "Hey, Frosh!
     You were at the wrong bus stop.
     Let me have your bus pass.
     Come on.
     Don't make me give you a wedgie
and a dirty swirly."

Because I have this pen and a single
pad of paper, I write as if all I had was
the words upon my back, and I set out
for the frontier on a government funded
expedition with cartographers,
geologists, and military scouts.
I'm in search of the seven cities of gold,
     on this space oasis,

aboard this moving bus called
"Life."

I'm sluggish, and my head is spinning.
I take the transfer and re-board the bus.
I'm a single protein on a roller coaster
artery, and I'm firing fantasies and
mysterious memories across my brain,
as I eavesdrop on conversations and
inhale exhaust fumes.
All these people going somewhere and
doing something
  when there is nothing to be done
  and nowhere left to go.

"Squeak, Vuvvvv-Ummmp."
The double doors open before me.
My stomach rumbles.
The end of another day.

The *Missing* Metaphor

In the January morning, he steps
delicate over ice blanketed
walks, fresh snow-covered medians,
and dog tracked lawns.
He bounces his basketball on the clear
concrete court of the community
center and misses shot after shot; as if
the basket is molded in bronze.

Finally, he follows the ball to the basket,
rebounds it, and throws it
back up. The ball bounces off the rim
then falls in but hangs up
in the still frozen net, as if it is part of a
sculpture.
Caught in a trap,
he looks at the ball just out of reach,
stuck, hard-set.

In the January morning, he jumps and
pops it up; then watches
the frozen net trap it six times in a row.
With a nearby orange cone, he pops up
the ball without jumping. It bounces and
goes back in again.

Cone in hand he pops it up and finally
frees the trapped ball.

Then at the top of the key; he's still no
better than before.
Scoring when he wants to miss and
missing when he wants to score.

A Parable for Our Time (revisited)

for Peter Michaelson and Carl Sandburg

A soda vendor on the side of 35th street
calls out
and the all the fans gather round
and buy him out and offer tickets.
They chant,
"Some things we buy, some not."
and scoop him and his empty cooler on
their shoulders
and walk him down to gate 5.

Another group mobs the ChiSox Grill.
People sit next to strangers;
the television mysteriously goes silent
and black
and suddenly strangers reach across
tables
and shake hands.
They sing along to classic rock
realizing they know all the words.

Despite his impulse to create
a wide berth of personal space
at the overcrowded bar, a stranger,
with his hair dreaded up tight,
resists the impulse to push away,

and tell another stranger that
he's crowding and too close,

He looks at the nondescript white guy
and instead of glaring
over his Bohemia and her margarita,
Hands him their menu as they've
ordered
and menus seem a little scarce right
now,
and says,
"Some things we buy, some not,"

He strangely feels the urge to get
acquainted,
to meet a stranger at a bar before the
game.
This new stranger is not even in town
that long and has no real interest in the
Sox
but he's hungry because he's been
bopping around the city and just simply
forgot to stop for food.

The beer is cold; the sun is warm; and
the fans fill every empty table before the
gates open and the crowd spills into
seats on a sunny picture-perfect day.

Routine

My muse eats breakfast,
shadows me from room
to room until she
senses that we are
indeed going for our
morning walk.
Some days,
I'm sure she doesn't
even really want to
walk but holds there
thinking that a walk
is really what's required.

It's all theory, but
late at night, my muse
stands sentry beside the bed,
and I judge,
"She needs to go out,"
but once I'm up,
she'll often just circle
back to her bed as
if she was just reminding
me of my routine.
"It's her routine," I think,
"because she needs out." And
"It's his routine,"
I think she

thinks, as she prompts me
to get up late at night.

At about five she'll start
bugging me for words, even though
I never type them before six
thirty, so I'm not persuaded that
this has become a pattern and
she frets that I'll forget if
she doesn't let me know she's
there. Quite often she'll give up,
so then it's a pleasant surprise
when I put my hands upon
the keyboard and just start
typing.

She'll come in, discover the
words and eat them, but she always
lets me know
when she is done.

More about Don McIver

-SIX TIME member of the ABQ slam
team as a poet and a coach

-Host/producer of KUNM's
Afternoon Freeform radio program

Author:
-The Noisy Pen The Blank Page
-Mud in the Stacks

Editor:
*-A Bigger Boat: The Unlikely Success
of the Albuquerque Poetry Slam
Scene.*

Also from Hercules Publishing

THE ART OF ESCAPE
by Trier Ward